EXPONENTIAL IMPACT

EXPONENTIAL IMPACT

HARNESSING HUMAN POTENTIAL TO DRIVE SUSTAINABILITY IN ORGANIZATIONS

AURORA DAWN BENTON

MANUSCRIPTS PRESS

EXPONENTIAL IMPACT
Harnessing Human Potential to Drive
Sustainability in Organizations

ISBN   979-8-88926-150-6   *Paperback*
        979-8-88926-151-3   *Hardcover*
        979-8-88926-149-0   *Ebook*

To the champions who tirelessly fight to change their organizations to be places where positive impact radiates.

CONTENTS

INTRODUCTION

"Am I the only one seeing this?"

Anyone on a journey of discovering their own thought leadership will ask themselves this question. The solutions seem so obvious. Surely everyone understands what I know to be true. As a new entry into an arena, you especially doubt you have tapped into some special secret.

This was me when I immersed myself into the sustainability discourse in 2016. My impression early on was sustainability could be easily summed up as elitist, esoteric, scary, and harsh. Never mind there's a fundamental misunderstanding of what sustainability is. It is seen as just light bulbs and electric vehicles rather than comprehensive impact in social, environmental, and economic spheres (also known as the triple bottom line of people, planet, and prosperity), as demonstrated in the United Nations Sustainable Development Goals, which include categories ranging from poverty and education to renewable energy and biodiversity.[1]

Like many setting out to be an expert in their field, I started with specialized and technical elements. Following nearly a decade of mentoring social entrepreneurs, I pursued a Doctorate in Business Administration in Social Impact Management. I performed a qualitative study of the barriers and facilitators to success for food manufacturing startups with social and environmental missions. These insights were later applied to a research effort I led on supplier diversity in the events industry, which culminated in a paper copublished by the Society for Sustainable Events.[2]

Years of focus on social impact left me out of balance given the broad nature of sustainability, so I dove into the environmental pool by earning certifications from organizations such as the International Society of Sustainability Professionals, US Green Building Council, and the Sustainable Furnishing Council. Armed with vast knowledge of the frameworks, acronyms, pledges, and science related to sustainability, I realized I was no closer to solving the real problem. Sustainability, simply put, was unapproachable.

I built a brand on making sustainability appealing and practical, toning down the language and framing it with some humor. Soon I won clients and got to put my revelations to the test. I experienced firsthand the potential of what I knew to be true: When you engage and empower anyone in an organization, they play a valuable role in delivering exponential impact.

I receive such satisfaction from observing a line-level employee demonstrating pleasure from participating in their organization's positive impact. Turns out, this experience is unusual; the norm is lower levels of organizations are disengaged and disenfranchised from sustainability strategy and programs (much less other meaningful initiatives). Staff feel detached from the heartbeat of the business. A connection to what brings life to an organization kindles belonging and thriving.

Even middle management is often waiting on others to give them permission to pursue a passion. They passively accept what superiors deem the direction for their career, yet that may not align with their values or hopes for the world. That disconnect drains energy and enthusiasm that could be funneled into making organizations great—not just in social and environmental impact, but in efficiency, innovation, and culture.

On the same note, it is difficult to engage and motivate lower levels and middle managers. Just because they have passion, and even if they get permission, it does not mean they will automatically respond in the most productive or effective way. Do they have a clear path to channel their interest? Do their attitude problems override any altruistic thoughts? Do staff discern a direct connection between their personal preferences and corporate objectives?

These observations made me curious about how sustainability evolves in organizations. In recent years, sustainability has exploded in the corporate world. You'd be hard pressed to find a major organization without an official sustainability role or even an entire department. The GreenBiz *State of the Profession* 2022 report revealed increases in CEO interest in sustainability, sustainability budgets, usage of sustainability consultants, and sustainability department size.[3] Much of this is driven by external pressures from stock markets, watchdog groups, and the growing base of eco- and social-conscious consumers.

For thousands of small and medium businesses, or larger privately held businesses who are not influenced by the investor demands for reporting on environmental, social, and governance (ESG), sustainability is still in the dabbling phase. It's informal and unformed, manifesting as a portion of someone's job who already had a staple corporate role (for example, a marketing director becomes the de facto sustainability charge because they are best suited to generate reports or a building manager becomes the *"green guy"* because reducing heating and cooling loads is a top priority initiative). No one has the official mandate for social or environmental issues outside of topics dictated by law (for example, health and safety, harassment). If no one is taking this on, then...well, no one is taking this on.

The same can be said for how sustainability plays out in a single location of a corporate brand. Just because headquarters is saying it doesn't mean folks on the ground are doing it. Most global corporations are beyond this as they have fully staffed sustainability departments; however, of the dozens of people I've mentored within such organizations, I repeatedly hear complaints that they are not feeling it in their daily routine. Corporate policies and programs may exist, but they don't see it play out around them. This leaves them feeling disappointed.

They feel left out because they are ready and willing to participate but do not see a clear path to involvement. I argue these larger corporations could benefit from returning to a grassroots approach, allowing champions to emerge and flourish anywhere they are in the organization.

In more than fifteen years of mentoring young professionals and conducting training in individual locations of corporate brands (for example, franchised hotel chains), I've witnessed how sustainability is birthed and nurtured in organizations. A person who is passionate for sustainability and tenacious and courageous enough figures out how to carve their own destiny. They raise their hand and step out in boldness, or they fly under the radar and quietly change their corner of the world. They often had the right teacher or boss at the right time, but sometimes it's just innate talent and will. These are exceptional people.

This book was inspired by the thousands, or millions, out there whose interest is below the surface, ready to burst forth if the right conditions are in place. In writing this book, I drew upon the dozens of students and young professionals I've observed and mentored as they took a spark of passion, or even outrage, about some social or environmental cause and began to forge a path for themselves and, perhaps more importantly, for their organization. Their energy and focus started to spread and at some point, leadership needed to take the reins. As great as this intrapreneurial momentum was, it does ultimately need to align with the overall mission and strategy.

How do we tap into that potential for the good of our planet? How do we create more of them and let them loose to transform organizations?

A fundamental failure of leaders and executives in tapping that potential exists. What I see is:

- Words without action:
  - o Corporate leaders launched sustainability initiatives for good PR without well-planned programs that generate consistent, measurable, and tangible impact.
  - o Corporate sustainability centered on policies without execution, reinforcement, or accountability. Furthermore, policies were written in a vacuum that doesn't account for the needs of stakeholders—namely employees who must comply.

- Inaccessible and unapproachable:
  - o Organizational sustainability was perceived to be the role of only a few—the elite, the capable, the specially educated and titled, which leaves out many with passion and energy to contribute.

o   Sustainability professionals often used too much blame and shame, and people ended up feeling it would never be enough so why bother. Fear and urgency without hope negated a clear path for others to follow.

- Organizational barriers:
  o   Corporate sustainability assumed doing the right thing was the perfect impetus, that noble causes beget noble actions. They ignored human motivation and behavior.
  o   People approached sustainability with an either/or mindset. Sustainability was generally pitted against something else, and those trying to drive it often see it as an imperative, but moving the needle required agreement from those who still see it as a choice.

Organizations fall short of their sustainability initiatives, employing *"because I said so"* approaches and a *"check the box"* mentality. I believe sustainability initiatives aren't achieving what they could because organizations have left a significant stakeholder—the champions, both visible and hidden—out of the equation.

If your organization is new to sustainability, it is highly likely your foray into social and environmental projects will start with a champion bold enough to walk you into unchartered territory. Some leaders and staff may resist this because fear of the unknown is a powerful immobilizer; however, you know you are already being left behind by competitors. If that resonates, this book is for you.

If you are a company executive, your sustainability initiatives may have been designed by some of the brightest minds in their fields; however, if you are not seeing the results and transformation you intended, the problem is not in the design. It's in the implementation. If that resonates, this book is for you.

If you are a young professional eager to see your career and values converge in the work of sustainability, you may be looking for a new job or to start an advanced degree in sustainability. You can drive change right where you are. If that resonates, this book is also for you.

Exponential Impact is presented in a series of four engagement and leadership principles. Chapters include application discussions and activities to put concepts into practice within your organization. I hope to see people take action. I don't mean activism, although that may be part of how this work manifests. I mean *engaging people* such that each person then takes small steps. This results in a cumulative and compelling program of exponential impact.

o   Part 1: The **Empathize** section is about engaging a variety of stakeholders and understanding attitudes and assumptions about sustainability. It includes chapters that break down different types of stakeholders:

- **Emphatize:** Lay the Foundation
- **Inside:** The Heart of the Matter
- **Outside:** People and Planet as Stakeholders
- **Up:** Executive Viewpoint
- **Down:** The Front Lines of Impact
- **Around:** Organizational Culture
- **Across:** Strength in Numbers
- **Across:** An Extension of the Family

o Part 2: The **Enlighten** section is about raising awareness, spreading knowledge, and providing instruction to those who need to carry out the work. The chapters are organized to answer classic questions:

- **Enlighten:** Precursor to Impact
- **Who:** It Takes All Kinds
- **What:** Campaign for Change
- **Where and When:** Getting the Word Out
- **How:** Stick the Landing

o Part 3: The **Empower** section is about ensuring all that listening and messaging leads to truly transformative change; it's about enabling the organization to walk the talk. The chapters reflect a progression that happens when sustainability starts out as an informal idea and evolves into a fully integrated element of the organization. The chapters are:

- **Empower:** Walk the Talk
- **Agency and Autonomy:** Champions Rise Up
- **Activation:** Rally the Troops
- **Acceleration:** Speeding up Sustainability
- **Actualization:** Holistic Integration

o Part 4: The **Encourage** section is about the fact that sustainability can be lonely and exhausting work, especially for those driven to see change. People need connection through community, motivation from a vision, and compensation for their efforts. This part includes:

- **Encourage:** Keep the Fire Burning

Whether this is your first foray into sustainability or you are a seasoned veteran in need of a fresh infusion of inspiration, I'm thrilled to be your guide through these chapters.

CHAPTER 1

THE SUSTAINABILITY SCENE

SETTING THE STAGE

"Where do I start?" is the most common question I get when I speak to audiences newer to sustainability. I expect this from those who work in small to medium or privately-owned enterprises where social and environmental programs are nascent if not downright nonexistent. However, I also hear this question from those who work in global corporations with sophisticated sustainability programs.

When I'm asked this question, I think, *"Job security!"* Seriously, what comes to mind is, *"What problem can I solve for them?"*

"Where do I start?" usually means *"Which of all the social and environmental initiatives should I do first? Is there a checklist I can follow?"*

They're focused on *"what."*

By *"what,"* I am referring to the full scope of sustainability, with so many categories of problems organizations can solve through their initiatives. This is best demonstrated in one of the most globally prolific frameworks, the United Nations Sustainable Development Goals (SDGs).[1] These seventeen goals and the underlying 169 targets cover the gamut of initiatives ranging from philanthropic giving to nonprofits who help those in poverty to recycling cardboard boxes in which shipments of supplies arrive.

Sustainable Development Goals—Provided by the United Nations[2]—*The content of this publication has not been approved by the United Nations and does not reflect the views of the United Nations or its officials or Member States.*

Not only does this show the array of sustainability opportunities, it also broadens the definition of sustainability. Most people I encounter who are new to it think it is only *"green."* However, notice the entire first row is all social and economic impact. This SDG chart clearly offers a comprehensive list of issues relating to equity, the environment, and the economy, also known as the triple bottom line of people, planet, and prosperity (or profit).

When selecting the *"what"* most relevant to an organization or community, one could reference only about a thousand blogs, checklists, and standards documents on the internet or, in some cases, their own internal sustainability department. Lack of checklists isn't the problem.

It's not even about deciding *"which is the right priority given our organizational mission and strategy?"* Or even *"which is the most important for the community in which we operate?"*

No, what paralyzes them is fear of getting it wrong, fear of failing (again, because many have at least tried something that didn't go as well as anticipated), and fear of adding to their already full plates.

They're inundated with choices and voices. As people explore the possibilities of what they could include within their work deliverables or span of control, it gets overwhelming fast. They request checklists thinking this will simplify their decisions.

I can support clients in prioritization, but the more pressing problem I want to solve is how to begin *and* stay on a sustainability journey. My mindset is summed up perfectly by Fernando Trías de Bes who wrote, "Better a mediocre idea brilliantly executed than a brilliant idea with mediocre execution."[3]

Sustainability is not about doing the flashiest initiative; it's about doing *any* initiative in a manner that delivers positive impact to people and planet.

I've studied just about every business framework and theory that exists. Business can be successful if one follows the prescribed process. In real life, though, it's not as neat and orderly. In theory you develop a strategy to support your mission, set goals, create a plan, and execute. A jumbled mix of these steps is more representative of most experiences.

Sustainability, that is the social *and* environmental issues relevant to an organization, unfolds in a similar fashion. It *should* be embedded in the mission, baked into strategy, addressed in goal setting, considered in planning, and executed effectively. What happens in most cases is sustainability initiatives spring up, then the champions who drive it start to set targets. It becomes apparent goals won't be reached if sustainability is not formally resourced and included in planning. Eventually, the right people understand it is a strategic imperative.

A client told me she benefits from reading books by corporate sustainability pioneers; however, she's frustrated by their assumption it happens in a theoretically ideal order. They mostly write from the perspective of a leader who founded or grounded an organization in a social and/or environmental mission from its inception. They ignore the reality of typical organizational scenarios where sustainability is still very much a peripheral *"do we have to?"* concept.

To be frank, what some of those newer to sustainability want answered are questions like: *"How can I get this stakeholder off my back?"* or *"What is most important to the prospective client we're trying to win?"* or *"What's the cheapest thing I can do to get credit for saving the world?"*

This may seem crass, but this is reality. I am often brought into a client's organization by someone who does not own the work moving forward, someone with altruistic motivations. Eventually we get into the territory of staff who feel more like, *"What do I have to do to check the box and make you go away?"*

For those who are sustainability professionals, you recognize this and struggle to overcome these attitudes daily. No wonder our work is so difficult!

"The front line of an organization is a gold mine of talent, ideas, passion, and action waiting to be extracted."

I've managed to be successful at transforming sourpusses into supporters, applying the principles I cover in this book. I go in understanding effective sustainability, especially the initiatives I work on, is one hundred percent contingent on staff connecting with the concept and embracing change.

We've made less progress in social and environmental issues than we'd hoped because we have not successfully nor fully engaged and included staff in sustainability programs. This book addresses other stakeholders, and no doubt they are critical; however, employees are the first line of defense. The front line of an organization is a gold mine of talent, ideas, passion, and action waiting to be extracted.

Employees are the central figures in the two most common scenarios for how sustainability plays out.

FIRST, LET'S SET THE SCENES:

- Sustainability newbies: organizations early on the journey. The spark can be an internal champion seeking to transform the company or it can be resistant leadership who's been dragged kicking and screaming by clients and other stakeholders demanding a degree of sustainability within their operations.

- Impact in waiting: organizations with established sustainability programs and reporting. They have departments filled with smart people building brilliant programs. Success is evident in larger infrastructure projects such as energy and water efficiency; however, their last-mile problem is in initiatives requiring behavior change and human buy-in.

THE CAST

Now, the primary actors in those scenes are:

- A champion self-selects and is a galvanizing force and a critical piece of the puzzle. They are an internal advocate for a social or environmental cause and light a fire! Unfortunately, ideas ignite, but then execution falters and the flame fizzles. These passionate employees are well suited to stir up interest but, due to lack of experience, skills, and resources, struggle to see it through. Burnout is also a factor.

- An unwitting manager is *"voluntold"* to do this on top of their normal job. The genesis is response to a trend (for example, diversity and accessibility, sustainable fashion, investor reporting demands). Eventually this unsuspecting staff member can't help but become personally vested in social and environmental programs. The road is a long and slow one. Their challenge is lack of support, even from those who tasked them in the first place, and a siloed vision of sustainability limited by their departmental context.

Both operate in a vacuum for a while. It's lonely work. They persevere...

Note I did not list sustainability executives and departments. They are of utmost importance; however, in the impact in waiting scenario, they are directors, set designers, and others behind the scenes. They establish strategy and policies, install infrastructure, sign pledges, form partnerships, analyze data, and publish reports. Despite their amazing efforts, a disconnect between what they do and execution at operational levels remains. Some are fortunate enough to have direct access to and influence over the front lines of implementation; however, to realize desired outcomes of their programs, they need those key actors to play a part. This book holds solutions to breaking through to them.

In the scenes and actors analogy, it would be easy to see the rest of the organization as extras. They must follow along, or at least comply, to be part of the sustainability intention, but they do not play key roles. I contend this is where we have missed the boat. We must recognize how vital they are to success. In this book, I present techniques and best practices for engaging and activating the people in your organization.

This book contains stories and examples representing this assortment of scenes and actors.

THE PLOT THICKENS

Most sustainability champions I've encountered had a personal epiphany that led to a change in their own practices. Consequently, they either became the self-appointed sustainability leader at work and introduced initiatives, or they were the person who raised their hand the first chance some type of sustainability project was even hinted at. For some, it was their personal experiences with racism or oppression.

For me, it was learning much of the world's chocolate supply still contains slave and child labor. According to the US Department of Labor, there are 1.56 million children forced to work in chocolate supply chains in Africa.[4] I saw images of children harvesting cacao beans and reports on how this chocolate ends up in the supply chain of pretty much every major chocolate manufacturer.[5] I had seen the Fairtrade label on candy bars which sparked my learning journey on the topic. Once I had this revelation, I made a personal commitment when buying chocolate bars, which was frequently, to only buy Fair or Direct Trade (other labels may include *"bean to bar"* or *"single origin"* along with some form of authentication through story or testimony). This was my personal agency exercised for a cause that mattered to me.

Once that internal flame flickers, we are eager to enlighten the world with our newfound knowledge and convert them to our passionate belief. This is where many advocates fail. Their messages are filled with vitriol, and no one wants to be preached to. From personal experience, I find it difficult to bite my tongue during the key chocolate seasons of Valentines and Halloween. I feel compelled to let others know they are supporting a global industry built on the backs of enslaved persons! But that sure does dampen the mood.

In a corporate environment, turning off a prospective audience is even more detrimental than annoying a few trick-or-treaters. The champions carrying the torch of sustainability may be ill-equipped to effectively formulate or deliver a message, much less create a strategy or implement a plan to drive desired change. This is often a function of where they are in their career or functional journey.

Sometimes I meet champions who were initially nudged by a superior. They were nominated to fill a role someone else did not want or they were thrown into the deep end by someone who had faith in them. Other times, they self-appoint and begin a process of stumbling around in the dark trying to navigate the organizational bureaucracy and politics required to drive such change.

Whether eager and willing participants or not, most of them had to create new pathways in their organizations. The fortunate ones encountered someone who was willing to empower them, to instruct them how to do their work in an official capacity, and to equip them with resources and tools to get the job done. Even without such support, champions made it far on passion alone; however, impact never realized its full potential as organizational barriers eventually blocked progress. Most of the latter examples ended up taking their skills and tenacity to other organizations ready to capitalize on their altruistic aspirations.

Regardless of the path from nascency to maturity of sustainability in an organization, there's always drama.

This is not easy work, and champions need balance, community, and appreciation.

The engagement and leadership themes of empathize, enlighten, empower, and encourage in this book are the pillars of the inherent trajectory as well as the formula for a better and more successful way to drive organizations toward exponential impact.

PART 1:

EMPATHIZE

CHAPTER 2

EMPATHIZE: LAY THE FOUNDATION

It all starts with empathy, the launching point of any good product or initiative. It's the essence of user or human-centered design.

My career began in the software industry with NCR's Human Interface Design Center. At the time, the mid to late nineties, their software methodology was cutting-edge, as was their approach to employees and users. The software engineers spent time with people working in factories in Mexico, for whom they were developing new training programs. They discovered employees had low levels of literacy and little exposure to technology. This inspired an intuitive design. Rather than words like *"start"* or *"submit"* we commonly see in software, the engineers borrowed icons and functions from a technological device known to the employees: a VCR. Yes, a VCR! Again, back then, in software, this was revolutionary.

I had been a programmer, so I knew how to solve technical problems, but I was always bothered by how most programs' interfaces and functions were not intuitive. Indeed, most were downright frustrating. The human-centered, empathy-filled approach was refreshing and has forever spoiled me rotten for how software should be designed and work.

IDEO, an organization known globally for its innovations in design, particularly human-centered design and solutions that address some of society's greatest ills, acknowledges this "is all about building a deep empathy with the people you're designing for."[1]

The current stage of sustainability reminds me of where we were with technology thirty years ago. People were just starting to use email and carry laptops. It was just starting to be an entire department in organizations and take over every function in a business. The rapid adoption of technology was fraught with resistance from those who felt threatened and confused.

Similarly, sustainability is now touching all aspects of an organization's strategy and operations. Such a transformation, even if it leads to an improved world, is not going to be a breeze. When change is introduced, many might resist for a variety of reasons (some of which can be quite personal or political); knowing where they are coming from is paramount.

START WITH SPEAKING THE SAME LANGUAGE

Have you ever traveled to a country where you didn't speak the language? Most likely before you ventured out, you learned at least a few phrases of that language. Maybe you did it out of respect for the locals, or curiosity and the sake of learning new things. Perhaps you did it for purely utilitarian reasons, like finding the bathroom or ordering a beer.

This same principle applies to convincing others to support sustainability. For example, I still frequently hear the excuse that sustainability costs too much. Selling sustainability to those who control the money is about appraising the strategic relevance and the business case for sustainability. When it comes to getting support for social and/or environmental initiatives, it's important to speak the same language as those you're trying to convince.

Finance people easily think in terms of formulas and acronyms that make perfect sense to them, while sustainability people are in their own bubble of acronyms. Each industry or corporate function has inside jargon. When I started my sustainability consultancy, I chose to focus on the hospitality industry, which meant I found myself in professional kitchens and banquet operations with terms I had to get used to.

Like learning a new language, some of it I acquired formally through research and some I pieced together from context. Like regional dialects within a country, I found something was called one thing in one operation and something else in another. For example, in event catering most teams in hotels and convention centers have a report created each night after an event—event recap, banquet summary, end of night report, and any number of other titles, not to mention formats. Turns out this is a key missed opportunity for improving both sustainability and client experience. It was necessary to know the intricacies of this document to speak the language of those I'm asking to do it differently.

When we use terminology and context unfamiliar to others, it can feel like a foreign language to them. It leads to misunderstanding, intimidation, indifference. The ideas of return on investment and sustainability still seem to be at odds, so we need translators who speak the language of both sides. Remember what it's like to be in that other country where you don't speak the language (or don't speak it well)? It requires being willing to look a little foolish, ask a lot of questions, and maybe rely more on pictures and gestures.

Let's approach conversations about sustainability in the same way, with an openness to doing whatever it takes to communicate a point. And find the bathroom!

John Broadway, a specialist in sustainability reporting and communications, explained Yogi Tea's approach to sustainability storytelling. He wrote, "The result of all this diligent measurement, often presented over hundreds of pages of meticulous reporting, is the removal of sustainability from the realm of common interest. Instead, it becomes a specialists' discourse....The fact that sustainability has direct and immediate impact for real people simply doesn't translate past the acronyms, graphs, metrics, standards, and numbers."[2] Yogi Tea's methodology stands in contrast and is illustrated in their sustainability report, which is a beautiful, approachable, visual storytelling journey of suppliers around the globe.[3]

It's not just how we talk about and present sustainability concepts and results. If we rewind back to the very design of social and environmental programs, we will have the right story to tell. Many sustainability initiatives (and this goes for most corporate and community systems and programs) are designed by a few specialists—usually at or toward the top of, or outside of, an organization—based on their assumptions, beliefs, experiences, knowledge, and goals.

A classic demonstration of this is numerous well water projects aimed at solving the severe problem of water availability and sanitation across the African continent. A number of these failed miserably and offered valuable lessons learned. The initial ideas and installations dreamed up and funded by Western engineers and philanthropists were a success, but many of these projects have infamously flopped in the maintenance and upkeep phases, leaving communities no better off than where they started.

A well-studied example is PlayPump, a system that required children to spin a merry-go-round device that would pump water out of existing boreholes. On the surface, this was brilliant—what a creative and fun idea. However, over time they encountered technical and social challenges, and many wells did not deliver.[4]

The Center for American Progress (CAP), when reporting on such projects, concedes human-centered design requires more time and resources and can lead to less scalable solutions.[5] Specifically, the CAP author characterized the problem as, "What could have been an innovative solution to a pressing problem failed because much more time and energy was put into sales pitches to Western donors than toward researching whether the idea would work on the ground in real-life conditions."[6]

Similarly, when corporate sustainability program design neglects the reality of the people and resources needed to make it successful, these ideas do not trickle down, seeping into the organization's culture and structure. One organization was embarking on a journey of creating a more inclusive and welcoming community among a dispersed, virtual staff. Even well into COVID when the transition to remote work was far along, the staff had not been equipped with updated technology. As part of an environmental initiative, I held a focus group with employees and quickly realized I couldn't even practice a key principle of empathy—listening! The participants did not have webcams or speakers, and most chose to remain in listen-only mode!

"When empathy is injected into initiative design, not only do we avoid failure, we generate exponential impact."

Listening, observing, and experiencing are essential, and these are prerequisites many organizations do not meet.

A starting point is embedding mechanisms that make feedback and input possible. When empathy is injected into initiative design, not only do we avoid failure, we generate exponential impact.

IT'S PEOPLE, NOT PERFECTION

Every organization, every business operation, is composed of people. Customers are people. Vendors, partners, competitors are people. Your ability to succeed is driven by your relationships with people. Building a core connection with people behind operations creates momentum and determines success. You won't relate to people if you don't first understand who they are, what they do, and what matters to them. Empathy is about meeting people where they're at. They always have a backstory and more to reveal. Empathy acknowledges that most decisions and behavior are based more on fear and self-preservation than logic.

Don't mistake empathy for perfection. What many may get hung up on here is if we listen to everyone, we have to make them all happy. When I worked in higher education, we had processes requiring input from students, teachers, parents, staff, and advisers. At first, we feared broad stakeholder inclusion because we equated consensus with permission. My boss reminded us consensus was not required. We collected input and feedback, synthesized it, drew conclusions, and made recommendations; however, complete unanimity was unrealistic. I remember this being freeing. Taking in a lot of feedback can feel like losing control, and when you're responsible for the outcomes, control can be important.

If your dominant thinking is to appease everyone, you'll be paralyzed and unable to make decisions. Personally, when I'm working in stakeholder engagement, I want to hear what everybody has to say and value what they add to the overall solution; however, everybody in the room will not be completely satisfied in the end. Obviously, you do not want to hurt or disrespect, but making them happy is not the job. Having empathy and aiming to please every single stakeholder would be a never-ending battle.

I worked with an organization with a wide variety of stakeholders—staff, government, industry (including multiple segments and ranging from micro to large enterprises), customers and prospects, nonprofits, academics, local residents, and global peers. We held a series of stakeholder events with multiple opportunities to provide input. The way we managed the challenge of addressing so many different, and even competing, demands was to constantly remind everyone what the organization's mission and purview was. This set clear boundaries around how the organization could realistically address any of the many woes stakeholders expected them to tackle.

For example, someone complained about what was taught in local schools. We pointed out that while a valid concern, it was outside the boundaries of what this organization could reasonably undertake. This helped dissipate the general moaning and complaining people were itching to air out. Once we got down to some sensitive issues directly affecting how this organization worked (such as the choice to use stock images in marketing rather than images accurately reflecting staff and the community), the conversation became more productive. It still didn't mean everyone was happy, but it put us in a better position to find common ground.

The idea we must please everyone is an innate human inclination. Indeed, one survey revealed 49 percent of adults self-identify as people pleasers.[7] On an organizational level, it's gotten worse. Cancel culture keeps everyone on edge and many people struggle to set healthy boundaries. In interviews I conducted for this book, I mostly spoke to those in the Millennial and Gen Z ranges, and I remember being struck, especially by the women, how willing they were to say *"f*** it!"* and walk away from something.

Consider data from WeSpire's "State of ESG Employee Engagement in Impact," which showed 42 percent of employees would quit their job to go work for a company making more impact.[8] The upper levels of corporations should be scrambling to figure how to accommodate this phenomenon, yet not enable bad behavior.

The *"I can just walk away"* possibility (which customers can do far more easily than employees) leads us to overcorrect and creates an expectation that everybody must be happy, or even can be happy, and that's impossible. You, your ideas, your organization cannot be all things to all people. Empathy is a process of integration and alignment, establishing an identity and setting boundaries.

EMPATHY REVEALS TRENDS

If you follow sound principles of sustainability, you employ a stakeholder-driven process that acts as an early alert system to potential issues impacting your industry, communities you operate in, and customers you serve. Employees are a valid source of input in this regard.

In years of teaching sustainability, I encountered countless examples of students with brilliant ideas or observations about their workplace. Insights just waiting to be discovered. Rarely were students engaged on the topic; their employers didn't even think to ask the questions I was posing. At the start of the class, students filled out a form containing fairly basic questions about their employer's social and environmental initiatives. To be expected, their responses were typically high level but sometimes even that was telling.

One that stood out most was safety procedures and training. I attended a restaurant and hotel conference in North Florida about a year after Hurricane Michael devastated the Panhandle. Many panelists mentioned a key revelation from this disaster: few businesses were prepared for a crisis at all!

From that point on I added a question on the form: Are you familiar with the safety procedures at your workplace?

The vast majority had no idea, had never been trained, and would not know what to do in case of an emergency. Interestingly, most of them were based in Florida, a state not unfamiliar with natural disasters.

This lack of training on fundamental topics extends to other impact areas. The GreenBiz's *State of Green Business 2023* report showed only about half of companies offer "on-camera" training on discrimination and harassment.[9] Given the legal risks linked to these issues, this is surprising.

Maybe not so surprising. No one wants to think about the potential of active shooters or tornadoes or discrimination lawsuits or other threats and risks. In the grand scheme of sustainability, these are issues organizational leaders must manage. SDG 16 includes a target to reduce violence,[10] SDG 13 speaks of resilience in the context of climate related disasters,[11] and SDG 5 tells us discrimination must end.[12] Those who bury their heads in the sand when faced with such issues cannot expect to predict, much less manage, the events that are knowable. Never mind how they respond to the unexpected.

Employees are an excellent starting place because the very act of engaging them speaks volumes about the authentic concern of their employer. Otherwise, the silence is deafening.

How often do you speak with your staff about sensitive issues that trigger discomfort (theirs, not yours) and ask for their direct input on the solutions? What sort of conversations are you having with your customers? Are you just asking them questions largely fashioned for confirmation bias or are you opening up a dialogue that generates potentially painful but cathartic revelations?

We sometimes skip the process of stakeholder research because it gets loud. It's a cacophony of opinions and judgments. Lots of voices do not immediately harmonize. It takes practice and time, but with appreciation of each voice, you can make beautiful music. Music that resonates and draws in, songs that soothe, heal, and move your audience.

As noted earlier, empathy adds time and resources to decision-making and design. It's safe to say, in light of the world we currently operate in, that's better than suddenly having to justify why your brand persists with polluting operations, racially stereotyped images (an example of SDG 10, Reduced Inequalities), oppressive systems, and harmful products. The fact that these things seem to take companies by surprise means they have not been listening. Voices with power and money can drown everything else out.

Empathy manifests in corporate trends that are a long time coming: inclusion, belonging, justice, diversity, accessibility. Corporations employ techniques such as listening sessions and bringing in specialist consultants who can speak the language and act as translators.

Stakeholder engagement and pressure can be like a game of chess. Dynamics between and among stakeholder groups create movements previously unconsidered or downright rejected. Movements cause shifts in strategy, intentionally or not, anticipated or not.

In 2020, consumers made it clear they didn't want racist images in branding. Among the products that underwent a brand renaming because they had slavery and racist connotations were Uncle Ben's, Eskimo Pies, Fair & Lovely, Dixie Beer, and Aunt Jemima.[13] Had people been saying for years *"I would buy your pancake syrup if only you would remove that inappropriate brand representation"*? No, but that doesn't mean a segment of the population wasn't offended or even hurt by this portrayal. We all now recognize these changes have been a long time coming, but they seemed to sneak up on many companies.

Shortly after Black Lives Matters reignited in 2020, a friend shared that some initiatives her employer had been involved in had, for years, been given terms such as *"economic development," "closing the technology gap,"* and *"diversity advancement,"* which were, in part, designed to address racial inequities. As she put it, those programs couldn't get funded if they specifically called out the race factor. Organizational leaders are associating these concepts under the general umbrella of sustainability, as set out in the SDGs. They are more open-minded given the growing awareness and popularity of such frameworks.

Companies are clamoring to shift their narrative. It's great they're waking up and catching up, but wouldn't it be better to be ahead of the curve and leading the conversation than to have an awkward, canned, and reactive approach? You can only do that when you are inviting, listening, absorbing, and assimilating other voices.

LAY THE GROUNDWORK

Empathy is the foundation for the rest of the leadership and engagement principles in this book. It's the starting point of your sustainability journey. From there you can successfully enlighten, empower, and encourage, but if you don't have empathy, I don't know how the others can be effective. For example, to enlighten, or raise awareness, we convey knowledge or spark interest in a way that grabs the audience's attention. To empower, we identify where the imbalances are and right them by formalizing sustainability and granting decision-making power to champions. To encourage, we motivate people, gauge what makes them tick, and figure out how to keep them around.

A common expression about sustainability is that it's a journey. We need a map to navigate the landscape of stakeholders we should engage. It is universally accepted that a critical part of engaging stakeholders is getting the right ones to the table or ensuring some form of research and representation of them. It is helpful to explore why each stakeholder deserves or needs to be included and heard.

For example, when speaking with clients' staff about office sustainability, I want to better grasp why they feel it's necessary to print long documents. I learn what will be important in the design of the solution. Ideally, I have this conversation in their office, point to a stack of papers, and strike up a conversation about what the document is, the importance of it in achieving their goals and tasks, and how they use the document exactly—did they just read it, share it, take it home, mark it up? Questions that get past the surface will elicit the best and most useful information.

One of my clients defended printing of collateral by explaining older customers still want printed documents. Because we had a group of colleagues in the conversation together, another person pointed out, "That's not as true as it used to be; we just keep using that as an excuse." Another of my clients recently shared he has a hard time processing edits to presentations without printing them out and using a pen to make notes. This is his habit and preference. He's a senior executive, so simply saying "don't print" isn't going to cut it. He proudly pointed out he went from using a red pen to a *green* pen. Hey, that's progress I suppose.

Begin with an empathetic mapping of stakeholders, then follow through with empathetic listening and empathetic design (of messages, job processes, etc.). This map should take you on a journey up and down the staff hierarchy as well as across bridges into the community and larger ecosystem of your organization.

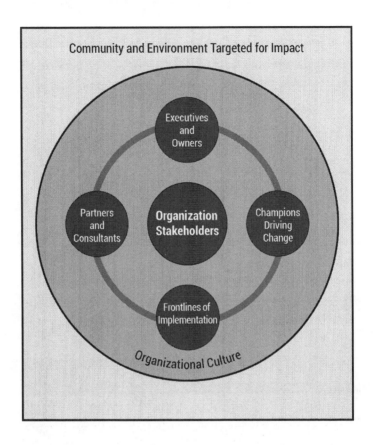

The Stakeholder Ecosystem for Empathy Planning—
Provided by Aurora Dawn Benton

In the following chapters, I take a directional approach to ensure we cover all the ground.

- **Inside: The Heart of the Matter** Empathy is an exercise in defining your own identity, as the champion of these causes or the group who aims to pursue a vision.

- **Outside: People and Planet as Stakeholders** These are the very stakeholders we are striving to protect, uplift, and improve in our purpose-driven work.

- **Up: Executive Viewpoint** The higher up the person, the more the authority, power, and accountability (in theory). Their sponsorship makes or breaks initiatives.

- **Down: The Front Lines of Impact** From line-level workers to supervisors and middle management, they do the work to carry out the vision.

- **Around: Organizational Culture** The history, staff attitudes, unwritten rules of engagement, and other organizational dynamics can pave the way or erect roadblocks.

- **Across: Strength in Numbers** Those who make up the rest of the ecosystem include clients, partners, vendors, and others who help or hinder along the way.

- **Across: An Extension of the Family** Specifically, consultants play a vital role in effectively designing and rolling out sustainability initiatives and, as such, should be granted access to stakeholders.

EXPONENTIAL IMPACT APPLICATION AND DISCUSSION

- What assumptions should you and your team challenge as you engage stakeholders?

- What judgments are others making that might impede your progress?

- What language do you need to learn to foster more effective conversations about sustainability?

- Which of your sustainability initiatives have fallen short of expectations? In what ways has the lack of stakeholder input contributed to the poor performance of the design or implementation?

- Draft a list of stakeholders to engage as it relates to a specific initiative or the overall sustainability program.

CHAPTER 3

INSIDE: THE HEART OF THE MATTER

KNOW THY TRIGGERS

I stood in line in a café in the small southern town where I reside. The person ahead of me ordered a soda, and the server handed him a Styrofoam cup (also known as styrene or polystyrene). This was one of those moments in which all my commitment and claims to make sustainability approachable and practical flew out the window.

I wanted to issue a shameful lecture right then and there on the evils of Styrofoam. It pollutes waterways and never fully breaks down; instead, it dissolves into microplastics both we humans and marine life ingest.[1] The Environmental Working Group scores styrene a 10 out of 10 (1 is best, 10 is worst) for its human health consequences, including its potential as an endocrine disrupter.[2]

When I launched Astrapto, I dove into all the online news and communities on sustainability. I noticed the overriding tone was negative. Blame and shame tainted sustainability news. I wondered if, rather than finger-pointing, we invited people to learn. What if, instead of focusing exclusively on urgency and crisis, we endeared people with positive images and possibilities?

I wanted to be a different voice in this crowd, but truth be told, I'm much better at being snarky. I realized I would have to make an ongoing conscious effort to fight my knee-jerk tendency to go to the negative and harsh. This is the classic *"fake it 'til you make it"* approach. It began to shape who I am and how I show up. It's a daily battle, and the good doesn't always win, but I accept that the cause demands it.

People don't give up methods deemed bad for the environment for several reasons. However, for many—on both sides of the argument and regardless how inane the motives—we are passionately devoted to our preferences. Anybody still serving food and beverage in Styrofoam is likely doing it because they don't know it literally never breaks down in landfills (it's made of petroleum so that stands to reason). They may not be required to make changes (by law or customer request), or they have tight budgets (it tends to be cheaper than alternatives). Styrofoam is just a part of everyday life and how dare you tell them it's a bad choice.

Meanwhile, I'm deeply triggered and seething when handed a plate made of this grotesque material! The person I want to be to drive change is at odds with the person I feel compelled to be in that moment. Every sustainability professional I've encountered has had moments of losing their cool over their hot-button issue.

"Every sustainability professional I've encountered has had moments of losing their cool over their hot-button issue."

The hottest of the buttons that trigger us likely bubble out of the deepest parts of our souls. As a kid growing up in the Deep South in the seventies and eighties, I was troubled by racism and what felt to me like backward ways of thinking and living. I spent my young adult years doing what I could to get out of the South. After I moved away, I lived in other parts of the country and the world for a few decades. However, I always struggled with being Southern, getting called out for my accent, worried people would think of me ignorant and backward.

For this and other reasons, it took me a long time to understand who I am, be okay with that, get in my lane, and own it like the badass I am.

A common thread among those I've interviewed over the years is this journey of self-discovery. Like me, they often find it necessary to create some identity distance from their roots. Their backgrounds do not spur interest in social or environmental issues. Although the desire might have been sparked by spending time outdoors with family as a kid and developing an appreciation for nature, a disconnect exists with their family on overall values of ecology and equity.

Those passionate about social and environmental issues can come at the world with angst, frustration, judgment, and criticism. It comes from a place of deep care and concern for people and planet and difficulty understanding why others would not share in that fervor, much less perpetuate the problems.

This thinking exacerbates the already polarized world we live in. In the 2023 *Edelman Trust Barometer*, a global study plotted countries in terms of how polarized their societies are. The US fell into the "severely polarized" category, while Canada and European countries were in the "moderately polarized" category but closer to the severe end than the less polarized end.[3]

It's easy to think this permeates our existence through and through; however, the study also showed among different types of people in our lives, there's a range of trust—government leaders scored lowest, while neighbors and coworkers scored much higher.[4] Personal relationships break through those surface generalizations.

We are complex and multilayered, capable of changing our hearts and minds, sometimes from moment to moment based on context. We see others through our own lenses, which have been tinted by our life experiences and assumptions. None of us sees perfectly clearly, despite how much we might think our eyes are wide open.

What's the baggage you bring to the table? What triggers you to feel vehemently passionate about a cause? What assumptions are you making about those on the *"other side"*? How might your zeal manifest as judgment?

Processing your own motivations is vital. Eventually you can help others examine their own and better express their desires and feelings, especially in a professional setting. The champion leading the cause, who is often a younger person still in those years that naturally bring about self-discovery, must ask, *"Who am I? Who do I want to be?"*

FROM CAUSE TO CAREER

Those who come to be champions of sustainability on an informal level are usually hoping to turn it into a career. This means knowing yourself on a personal and a professional level so you know where and how you can best serve the cause. Any career in sustainability will lead to making an impact. Recognizing your innate strengths and abilities helps you identify the positions where you will likely have exponential impact!

When I launched Astrapto in 2016, I was going through a phase of reflection that informed the brand I built. I had experienced a layoff and was soul searching for my next move. I was gifted a book, *The Confidence Code: The Science and Art of Self-Assurance—What Women Should Know.*[5] That was a revelation. I decided to follow my heart and work full-time in corporate social responsibility, something I'd wanted to do for many years.

It dawned on me: *"Whose permission am I waiting on to pursue my dream?"*

I embarked upon a journey of tapping into the feminist and power in me I had subdued for years. Many women of my generation have traversed a similar path at some point and that's certainly true among my contemporaries in the field of sustainability. We wanted to manifest change in the world and realized any part of our inner lives holding us back must be dealt with.

I also found it helpful to revisit my natural talents and strengths. Throughout my career, I've taken many style and personality assessments. (Organizations use these in recruitment and development, so many people have access to something like this. Even if you don't, free and affordable ones are available.)

Several years ago, I took CliftonStrengths[6] and found this assessment very helpful for affirming what I excel at and what I need to compensate for through partnerships. I asked my team members to join me in this exercise to better ascertain what work they enjoyed, what value they brought to the table, and how we could best collaborate.

CliftonStrengths validated what I already knew. I am strategic, an excellent communicator, action-oriented, and convincing. However, it also showed me why some tasks I thought I should be good at were difficult for me. I'm not hardwired to do certain things as well. I started identifying and partnering with others who possessed the abilities I lacked.

For example, one of the CliftonStrengths themes is Relationship Building. Most of the strengths in this theme are in the bottom half of my list. Conversely, the Influencing theme dominates the top half of my list. I joke, this means I like telling people what to do, but I don't want to get to know them. Ha!

Obviously, I am capable of being friendly and building and nurturing relationships, but this revelation helped me comprehend and manage why I struggle with the chitchat people seek after I deliver a presentation. I've learned how to navigate this so I don't offend others and don't end up drained.

Sometimes such revelations mean walking away from what should have been a good fit. I met Meena after she left a career as an attorney to immerse herself in purpose-oriented work. She sought alliance between her passion and talents. This landed her in a temporary position with a nonprofit she hoped to help, but ultimately she had to part ways.

Meena told me about her wise choice to do so. "As I got in there, I realized I didn't know if I was a culture match. I'm passionate about this, but there are expectations of those I'm coleading with on the inside that are not in alignment for me. After we got things rolling, I had to go back to the leaders and say, 'Listen, I have to step back from what you've asked me to do.'"

One of the hardest things for an advocate of social and environmental causes to do is own up to their fallibility.

We are superheroes. We may not always self-identify in this way, but that's the role we are trying to play. Being part of a team can expose weakness because we feel the need to be all things to all people. We should be vulnerable with those around us for the good of the cause.

Meena continued, "I told them, 'I can't lead this way, and you may need someone else. And that's great; it's just, I don't work that way. I'm slow and intentional.' They wanted fast-paced, drop-everything, get-this-done hustle. I can't. That's not who I am. This frees them up to be on the path they need to be on to accomplish what they're trying to accomplish. No hard feelings."

The better you know yourself, own your weaknesses, and lean into your strengths, the more effective you will be as a change agent.

THE TEAM TAKE

As my team grows, I have to teach others how to live out the brand identity I strive for. We want desperately to help our clients and see change in the world, but we must practice what we preach and recognize their journey may be slower and messier than we'd prefer. As a team, we have each other for sessions of commiseration and whining, which helps us work through our approach, tone, and deliverables.

If you're fortunate, you are embarking on this sustainability journey with a small team—either a green team or organizational leaders who are together committed to the vision. It's hard to process what you hear from stakeholders when you cannot decide who you are or how together you will show up in the organization. Whether a team is handpicked or sort of forced together, you have an opportunity to define who you are as a team in an intentional and overt way.

Sustainability is confusing enough for most people, so if you are not cohesive as a unit, it will be difficult for others to be inspired and follow your lead. As a team, collectively you will have quite a laundry list of initiatives and causes to pursue. Each person has their individual contributions and perspectives but convene and synchronize for exponential possibility in what you can do together.

The team dynamic brings strength-in-numbers comfort. Sustainability requires boundary setting and saying "no" to things many think are an obvious "yes". It's about sticking to a set of goals and a plan, which means some ideas don't make the cut and constructive criticism may be required to keep programs on track. The more confident you are in your style, strengths, and purpose, the easier it will be to lead others without defensiveness or frustration. The more your team has a unified charter and vision, the more unswerving you will be in establishing those boundaries and moving initiatives forward.

I liken this to a brand because in theory a brand defines how a company shows up in the marketplace, evolves products, seeks customers, and attracts employees. I recommend as you build a team (and remember, a team can consist of only two people), take time in your meetings to explore your sustainability identity.

The more clarity you have in who you are as an individual, as a champion, and as a team, the sooner you will start hearing what stakeholders want and seeing what they need. You will be more collaborative and in service to something for humanity, the company, the stakeholders, the community, and the environment.

EXPONENTIAL IMPACT APPLICATION AND DISCUSSION

- Share the origins of your interest in social and environmental issues with your team.

- Take an assessment and discuss how the strengths and styles can be best leveraged in driving positive impact. I mentioned CliftonStrengths, but there are many others available.

- If you have a green team (or whatever you might call your sustainability team), how would you describe the identity or brand of the team? In many organizations, green teams eventually dissipate because someone who was the glue holding it together left. Is your team cohesive? If not, be intentional about team building and conversations that tighten your bond as a group.

- If you have a team already, take time for each person to express their preferred roles and responsibilities on the team. What strength does each person have that can be tied to the success of social and environmental initiatives? Some people seek membership on such a team because of an altruistic passion; however, they have not given much thought to how it takes form in daily tasks. Others have been assigned to the team and may lack background or a particular position on causes. Explore what tugs at their hearts, tap into their natural talents, and leverage their style to find the right team role.

CHAPTER 4

OUTSIDE: PEOPLE AND PLANET AS STAKEHOLDERS

LISTENING TO COMMUNITY AND ENVIRONMENT

Throughout this book, you'll pick up on the theme that those who lead sustainability in their organizations often self-selected and volunteered. They came from backgrounds that didn't exactly prepare them for the full scope of their roles. Passion carried them far; however, even champions reach their limits. One way this plays out is in the design of social and environmental initiatives. These champions usually start with an epiphany that compels them to do more, but they lack the scientific and technical know-how to properly implement their ideas in a way that doesn't also create new problems.

If you are already a sustainability fanatic, it's easy to spot the problems and wonder, *"What were they thinking?"* It's more a factor of too many moving parts and inexperience in planning and executing community service projects and volunteer activities. For example, as sustainability has grown in popularity, conference and trade show organizers have added features and happenings to showcase social and environmental efforts, including projects attendees can participate in while visiting the host community. Examples include planting trees or preparing meals at a soup kitchen.

Marsha works in the events industry and knows conferences as both one who hosts and plans them as well as one who attends them. As a sustainability advocate, she's on the lookout for ideas to make exponential impact for attendees and the host community. She told me about an event offering an opportunity to paint murals at a local school. This is a popular design for a service activity because it's low-risk, fun for participants, and beneficial to the community. It may not transform the neighborhood, but it communicates to residents that someone cares. It gives onlookers a moment of joy in their day.

Marsha explained that after they finished painting, she asked for buckets to clean the water-based paint off the brand new, barely used brushes so they could be left behind as an added perk for the school. The service coordinator said, "Oh we have unopened paint brushes we'll donate so we're just going to throw out the ones we used today."

Insert major eye roll here! I hear stories like this all the time, but it never stops shocking me. Marsha refused to let it go at that. She went around and collected the brushes and found a way to wash them.

The stories I hear about impact-oriented activities leave me feeling these undertakings (sometimes known corporate social responsibility, or CSR) are designed more for the benefit and enjoyment of the people doing the action than the people supposedly on the receiving end. Beneficiaries are not considered sufficiently. On the environmental side, people get enthusiastic with ideas like, *"oh, let's use this straw made of so-and-so material"* or *"let's do this thing where we put the oyster shells back in the bay."*

These ideas are discussed with passion and creativity but lack scientific or operational reality. Did we talk to a marine specialist to make sure putting oyster shells in the bay is the right thing for the local wildlife? Is the bio-based material in the straw the best to end up in the ocean? I get that it's better than plastic, but we might throw off nitrogen balances that kill reefs or other such nuanced impacts of our well-intentioned good deeds. We must ensure we're not just doing this to make ourselves feel good; rather, we need to truly bring solutions to the world.

Social impact is often meant to address those in society who are most vulnerable. This requires you to know where someone's coming from and what their struggles are. To listen to people in a heartfelt way and comprehend their circumstances, empathy is necessary. Furthermore, when you are solving problems others are apparently facing, are you doing so with or without their input? Were they asked to the table? You might not know whom to invite; however, they're having problems, they're impacted, and somehow you need to represent them and their needs.

Some sustainability programs start out more apropos to those who can afford the higher costs of services and equipment. For example, a waste management plan could be designed to best fit a scenario where everyone lives in the suburbs, houses are large and somewhat close together, but yards and space are still ample. What happens when the same ideas are applied in the inner city where everyone lives in apartments and streets are narrow? What about those who live on rural county roads with no sidewalks, and only two or three houses exist in a one-mile stretch? The design of bins, trucks, routes, and schedules need to take all this into consideration. Were any of these audiences consulted along the way? Does anyone care what the experience will be for the single mom in a high-rise or the elderly farmer when it comes to complying with new programs?

It's okay if the initial rollout of a program works in mainstream residential or commercial environments. They have financial incentives and can pay the bill of scaling ideas and making it more economical for the rest. Let's pilot the program and fix the problems with those who have the funding and capacity. Then we roll it out broadly, as long as we haven't left other audiences to the side. We must get to a point where we can accommodate their scenario, and it's better to design that in early rather than unravel it later and retrofit for other stakeholder groups. Our vision may not be fully realized today, but we have a clear and workable vision for a point in the future.

While this approach is acceptable, it's important to consider how employees executing these programs perceive them. Once I go in and start talking about solutions to waste problems, I find staff have strong opinions and frustration that more is not being done. They do not have the full context of local infrastructure or operational realities. On the other hand, their fingers are on the pulse of community ails in a way that gives them intense empathy. Realities be damned, they just want to know why businesses aren't doing more or better to fix things.

SYSTEMS VIEW

Sustainability is inherently a complex system. Linking the environment to human health or activities people care about shows the interconnected nature of social and environmental issues and the intertwining of all aspects of life on earth. Too many of us are ignorant of overall ecosystems and the disastrous ripple effects of basic decisions made on personal, corporate, or governmental levels.

Something so lovely and innocent as buying a bouquet of flowers for a friend can be fraught with sustainability dilemmas. Consider the social, economic, and environmental implications of the cut flower supply chain. The US is a top importer of cut flowers, most of which come from Colombia and Ecuador.[1] Kenya is a major exporter of roses particularly.[2] These nations have inequities in this sector. For example, women make up most of the industry workforce and are frequently subjected to human rights violations such as sexual harassment.[3] Cut flower workers, who sometimes include children forced to work in fields, are exposed to a high degree of chemicals and poor working conditions.[4]

Flowers decline rapidly in quality and value once cut; therefore, they are often shipped via air freight and/or need refrigeration during transport. Both factors add to emissions generated.[5] The short lifespan of flowers means they quickly become waste. The heavy use of pesticides and herbicides pollute waterways, degenerate soil, and damage habitats.[6]

I opened this book with my proclamation to make sustainability approachable, but that doesn't mean putting our heads in the sand on these issues. Once we allow this knowledge to seep in, we can begin changing our habits. The approachability comes in with, well, the approach! Sustainability necessitates an ecosystem perspective, but it's not realistic to start with such a complicated viewpoint of a problem. That might be ideal, but action is stalled while we seek to analyze the entire system, become overwhelmed with sadness, or resist the idea this means giving up expressions of appreciation through flowers. We must offer viable and attractive solutions. In this case, buy flowers from local nurseries, opt for longer-lasting plants over cut flowers, and choose gifts produced by social enterprises.

The very nature of systems is they are ever shifting, which means you can't fully know all the answers. Only by starting, asking, engaging, listening, and evolving can you insert yourself into this system to better empathize and perhaps predict its next move.

Make stakeholder engagement an ongoing effort. The launching of sustainability initiatives includes a phase for stakeholder conversations; however, this task quickly falls by the wayside and, months later, stakeholders are left asking, *"Was there follow-through?"* Work may indeed be happening but, for those stakeholders, the conversation simply stopped. Create space for dialogue and listening on a regular basis, at least annually but more often if the initiative's success or impact dictates. Systems evolve, so ensure ongoing updates and communication about progress. Interaction with stakeholders is an interchange that continues and advances.

Take it a step further. Connect staff with stakeholders. Employees are part of the system. Normally listening exercises and stakeholder interactions are the domain of executives, specialists, and consultants. Why not allow lower levels of the organization to sit in on these conversations? It's unconventional to be sure, and probably uncomfortable because it's hard to control what staff might say or how they might respond. It's a risk, but it's a powerful way to tap into the passion, energy, and insights of the workforce.

IN THE TRENCHES

When connecting with community and environment, it's paramount to engage organizations who work face-to-face with these constituents every day. The *"constituent"* may be a body of water or a local habitat, in which case research centers and academic institutions house the experts who understand the problems and advance solutions. Our efforts are likely for populations with whom we lack experience. We wouldn't know their unique settings and needs. Outside organizations can magnify an organization's CSR investment using its special knowledge and access. For example, Subaru, through its Subaru Love Promise CSR program, partners with Operation Warm, an organization that supports the social and emotional needs of children.[7] This ensures Subaru's precious resources are funneled into the causes they most desire to support.

In a food waste program at a convention center, we took a group of employees to visit the local food donation partner, a center providing housing, food, and recovery services to vulnerable residents. Kitchen personnel had complained the community partner would *"cherry pick"* and not take all the food they had left over.

On the tour, I asked the nonprofit director why that would be. He expounded on a number of reasons. Every day, they feed lunch to about sixty people who live on the street and thirty people in their recovery housing. The organization needs to have enough food to give everyone the exact same meal because if people sitting at the same table have different foods, fights break out.

Whoa! He went on to explain they can't serve foods requiring a knife...per the aforementioned fights. They can't serve foods with seeds, nuts, or bones because their patrons have dental issues (essentially missing teeth) caused by substance abuse. I've been working in food waste for years and pushing my clients to donate food, but I've spent little time on the food donation side. I've been to and volunteered in food banks and soup kitchens, but I'd never directly connected these technicalities with my work.

Honestly, I was most impacted by the director's explanation, given it was practical advice I could apply in my food waste work in other cities. The staff were far more moved by other elements of the recovery program and its impact, such as the success stories of residents. The next day in the training session with the larger group of staff, each of us shared what had stood out. Some were nearly in tears as they described what they witnessed and learned. That was an absolute game changer in the staff's commitment to new programs and improved processes to reduce food waste.

Another example comes from a champion I interviewed. Chance oversaw sustainability at a convention center. He shared his experience learning about problems in their community. "We engaged with nonprofits that are trying to solve these problems. They have the mission, and they're on the front lines of those issues. They became strategic partners who allowed us to understand what the issues were and how we were negatively contributing to those issues."

Nonprofit organizations working closely with the community can share insights and offer ideas and innovations to solve the problems we cause. It's difficult to grasp the negative consequences of our operations from our daily bubble. Community partners are our eyes and ears on the ground to convey the reality of life outside our little world. Convention centers generate tons of waste and when properly channeled, that waste can become art supplies, theater props, and other creative utilization of the myriad items moving through the building.

However, don't expect to walk away with a one-time fix. Chance explained how the efforts to solve problems perpetuated existing challenges. "All these materials come in from trade shows and go out to the nonprofits to support their work. They were so excited and would take all sorts of weird things and then try to find solutions, but eventually it becomes a burden because stuff is a burden. We created bottlenecks because there was so much material. I always knew that was coming, but I had to solve one problem to get to the next one."

A typical path in sustainability starts with managing waste we create, which typically results in a focus on recycling and composting. The journey Chance described is finding better streams for waste through repurposing and reuse.

The next frontier is to proactively eliminate waste. New and different partnerships will be required, such as working with startups innovating trade show booth design, collaborating with distribution and shipping companies to extend the life cycle of booths, and convincing exhibitors to do their part.

The benefits of partnership are a two-way street. These scientific and community organizations can offer their technical know-how, but they may lack the resources corporations bring to the table. Businesses have know-how in marketing and communications, financing and managing projects, and other functional capabilities that may serve the nonprofit community. When engaging these entities, be sure to fully explore what they need from you and be transparent about what you need from them. It could be a match made in heaven.

EXPONENTIAL IMPACT APPLICATION AND DISCUSSION

- What are the top environmental issues where your organization operates? Start with a broad, general list and then narrow down to causes that align with the mission and priorities of your organization or green team.

- What are the most pressing social problems in surrounding communities? Check in with staff on their perceptions of these issues. Ask them to contribute to the list by sharing what they see and experience in their neighborhoods.

- Who are the nonprofits and community partners who can provide access to and insights about key community stakeholders?

- What conservation organizations operate in your area?

- What scientific or academic institutions can help you better assess the relevant environmental issues?

CHAPTER 5

UP: EXECUTIVE VIEWPOINT

EXECUTIVES AND OWNERS

Sustainability is a waiting game, and ninety percent of that is waiting on executive approval to move forward. I'm a person of action, so this drives me nuts. I don't dispute executive buy-in is critical. Important yes, but sufficient no. Organizations underutilize and overlook their lower-level employees. However, since we do need, and greatly benefit from, upper levels of approval, let's start there.

One of the problems we, as sustainability professionals, must own, is we have not always done a great job of appropriately engaging executives and owners. I don't mean *"kiss the ring"* appropriate, I mean *"speak the same language"* appropriate. Many of those I interviewed had similar experiences of learning how to engage executives and sell ideas up. Since many who get their start in sustainability begin at entry-level roles or volunteer positions on a green team, they come in with a bit of naivete and do not see eye to eye with executives.

Ellen's story was quintessentially representative of so many I have heard over the past decade. She convinced the owners of a restaurant chain to create a sustainability position for her. They were truly committed to positive impact as a central part of their company. In this new capacity, Ellen started attending meetings with the executives.

She shared, "As much as we didn't really want to admit it, decisions were driven by financials and profitability. At first I was like, *That's not important.* I missed the business piece. I wanted us to be radical and just do environmental work. Then I realized, *Hold on, I'm not reaching everyone in the room, so how can I get the message across?* I had to do a lot of reflection about the role of profits. If we don't have that, we can't generate positive impact in the way we want."

For me and probably many reading this, that revelation may seem like *"no duh."* However, see this through Ellen's eyes, the viewpoint of someone super excited about living out her values of sustainability. She's been given the green light for a full-time position in sustainability. She's young, eager, and inexperienced. Of course she's going to get ahead of herself.

Given how often sustainability initiatives start informally with champions like Ellen, I implore corporate leaders to proactively engage them. This is reverse empathy in this case, but the owners and stewards of the business should maintain the highest level of accountability to ensuring sustainability champions—or anyone leading innovation for that matter—are properly educated on how the business operates and turns a profit.

The reality though is it will largely fall into the hands of sustainability champions to learn this on their own, and probably the hard way through a lot of rejection, negotiation, and persistence.

I believe so many say executive buy-in is essential because it can greatly reduce friction from other parts of the organization. When the person at the top sets the tone that conveys *"sustainability is not a priority,"* it comes through loud and clear, even through some passive-aggressive and avoidance behavior.

I was on a client site presenting findings and recommendations from a four-month long effort to develop a sustainability blueprint. We were set to present to the executive committee. Going in that day, my colleague commented about a senior leader being in the meeting. I replied, "I bet he won't be there." She had a shocked look on her face. I said, "No, he's going to find a reason not to be there. There will be some fire drill."

I wish I'd placed money on that bet. Not only did he have some pressing matter preventing him from making any part of the meeting, he also conveniently finished his other business right at the conclusion of our session, at which time he walked by, motioned to an executive in the room, and pointed to his watch to indicate it was time to head out for their lunch appointment. It is tough to include a stakeholder who won't give you the time of day.

This indifference was exasperating for staff who invested substantial time and effort developing a sustainability strategy. They felt stuck, not sure how to proceed. Decisions and communication regarding next steps were on hold without a clear nod from the man at the top. Lip service is sometimes enough to get things going, but one staff member in this organization told us outright he felt our work was just another shiny object and a year later nothing will have changed.

ADVOCATE OR ADVERSARY?

While someone at the top may erect barriers, once they're on board they can bulldoze through obstacles faster than anyone else. I can report that persistence paid off and that executive who wouldn't give us the time of day is now leading the charge with bold commitments. This sets the tone, inspires action, and drives exponential impact!

"While someone at the top may erect barriers, once they're on board they can bulldoze through obstacles faster than anyone else."

I've heard many stories of champions turning adversaries into advocates.

Valerie leads sustainability efforts for an entertainment company and deals directly with C-suite decision makers. She won over a resistant leader. "This is often my biggest challenge, the CFO or the person who is responsible for making sure the event is profitable. That's my nemesis, but I have developed a relationship with this person, and they now get it."

I know firsthand a couple of sentences does not begin to do justice to how much patience and convincing it takes. It's like the saying *"death by a thousand pinpricks,"* except in a good way. It's letting in the light one little pin hole at a time. That's why Valerie's next statement was, "That's my biggest win, honestly, seeing this person take me and the program seriously and how it impacts the bottom line, whether through profits or brand equity and marketing value."

Over time, you pick up on patterns of how to best address executives and convince them to give your ideas time on the agenda, much less give them credence or allocate resources. I dislike it, but I have come to terms with the fact that executives have, whether rightfully earned or just granted via their title, certain expectations about the world around them bending to their needs and will. If too rigid in your approach, you are not likely to get through to those top stakeholders.

Valerie figured this out. "The hardest part is making them understand what it is I do that is of value to them. It changed how I approach the person in that position. I learned to practice mirroring, and I find it helps. If somebody's dry and straight to the point, like most executives I deal with, they don't need the story or the details, so I speak to them in bullet points."

Ellen, who I referenced above, struggled with this, but ultimately, she broke through while maintaining identity. "In the beginning, I was not as confident. My mentor gave me feedback and said when I speak, it's too esoteric. He's our financial lead, a straight-to-the-point guy. At first, I was like, yep, too esoteric. I will try to cut back and speak in bullet points."

The sustainability champions, especially younger ones, must find their voice. Accommodating someone else's style can feel like wearing the wrong size shoes. You're going to come off unprepared, inauthentic, maybe even clumsy. Championing an idea requires the kind of conviction derived from being our true selves.

Ellen was not able to make that adjustment to her approach but was able to justify why her job requires a different style. "Even if I had a presentation with bullet points, I couldn't. I would start speaking, and my heart would pour out. I remember thinking my job is to get in at a different angle. I told him, I think this is great feedback, and if I'm doing a high-level update, that's fine, but if I'm trying to explain *why* we're doing something, I can't do my job well if I can't use my words."

The common thread in both Valerie and Ellen's stories is relationships. Executives, just like other stakeholders, are not a one-size-fits-all category of people. Yes, they are primarily focused on the bottom line because that's part of their job and that's pressure they constantly deal with. Their time is precious, and they often express intolerance for details and backstory. However, they are human and didn't get to where they are without some experience managing people and expectations.

The way we go about approaching executives can make a difference, even when no relationship has been established. Donna worked in a factory and had rare and limited access to the national executives who could sponsor her ideas. She determined the business case for her priority initiative and started there. She laid out costs and revenue projections. Once they were in love with the idea, she added in, "Oh, by the way, here's how many trees we save, the reduction in carbon emissions, and the reduction in waste to landfill." Unfortunately, if presented the opposite way, projects aren't accepted as easily by management.

Executives and owners ultimately own the vision and strategy. Sustainability must align with and enhance these, not take over. A business can shift its entire strategy based on sustainability, but this is uncommon and plays out gradually over time. When first pitching ideas to these stakeholders, it helps to find the ways your program would support what's already important and prioritized.

Over the years, I have served on a variety of industry association sustainability committees and task forces. One of those was an organization led by a group of people, especially the guy at the top, who were vehemently opposed to sustainability. They pulled no punches on this topic. In fact, on one committee call, the CEO was emphasizing how important it was we align with their stance against a proposed environmental legislation. I reassured him our goal was to focus on the possible and positive. In other words, we were ready to pick our battles and focus our efforts and messaging on safer territory where we would more likely win people over.

He came into the meeting convinced we'd be a bunch of tree-hugging pains in the butt. We didn't get credit for grasping the delicate nature of this situation. Yes, we would all have loved to see this legislation passed, but we were realists. His patronizing tone and the lack of professionalism was shocking. I had rarely experienced something so blatantly chauvinistic and childish in the corporate world. What could have been a helpful, strategic conversation led ultimately to resignations, board problems, and bad press.

Contrast this with the CEO of United Airlines, Scott Kirby, who has been recognized for his stance on sustainability at a time when airlines were not exactly making this a front and center topic. When it comes to discussions about carbon emissions in tourism and events, naturally the elephant in the room is flights. You can't really experience growth in these areas without more people getting on more planes. In the earlier days of this movement, most of the airlines either ignored the environmental problems or they had a small internal faction working on it but by no means was it the brand differentiator it has become.

According to an article in Triple Pundit[1], Kirby has been outspoken on the realities of carbon emissions in the aviation industry. In an era when so many CEOs are doing all they can to sugarcoat with sustainability speak, it is refreshing to see a leader willing to go after it head on instead of head in the sand. Not only is Kirby known for his push for sustainable aviation fuel and other (in theory) realistic and effective environmental solutions, he has also been called out for his efforts to create a positive culture.

Is he perfect? No. Plenty of journalists, employees, and customers have something negative to say. From what I've read, though, I'll take his leadership over the other executive I spoke of any day. We should be careful about expecting perfection. Hold people accountable, but still empathize the CEO of a global corporation is going to have off days.

WINNING THEM OVER

Not every antagonistic executive is going to self-destruct, so for a while you may find yourself needing to interact with and convince a naysayer at the top. Ultimately, having empathy for stakeholders who hold the most power in an organization includes understanding:

- Pressures they face and who they answer to. How could your ideas alleviate stress? How would your ideas potentially exacerbate it? That person I had a negative experience with was responding to a fear that sustainability limits the growth of an industry he was tasked to support through governmental advocacy.

- Macro trends, regulations, and other external situations demand their attention. How does your sustainability initiative positively respond to these? Have you done your homework to know the landscape and ensure your initiative fits the situation?

- Bubbles they live in. Let's face it, most people at the top, even if they came from humble beginnings, live in a world of privilege. Even those who support charity or are minority, women, or LGBTQ will have myopia in their perspective. How will you get them to look outside their own reality long enough to see the problems you want to solve?

- Language they speak and respond to. We'll get to this more in the section on Enlighten, but when you are in empathy mode, listen and watch for the cues that reveal the words, images, and concepts you can leverage to message your ideas.

- Personal experiences connecting them with a social or environmental issue. Even if they live in a bubble of privilege and can't see the true woes of the world, they are people. They like to garden, hike, sail, cook. They have kids, pets, partners. They have heartstrings that can be tugged. What have you done to learn about their personal likes and lives (while respecting privacy)?

It does not mean you or your message bend to all these points. It's about context, not conformity. The message is more likely to land and the idea take off if the executive is compelled to sponsor it. The list above is the undercurrent of their philosophical perspective, but we must also get practical. Too few executives at the top know exactly how sustainability optimizes business performance, opens new markets, mitigates risk, and improves culture. Sustainability is enough of a trend most will acknowledge the organization should be doing *something*. Put that something into concrete terms with a clear business outcome.

The adage *"money talks"* is apropos here. Ask questions and listen for clues relevant to the business case of sustainability. This is a bit of a chicken and egg dance. You may not have enough input to yet know which initiative is the right one to start with, but it can't hurt to take an educated guess and go through the exercise. You're going to win them over by speaking their language and recognizing their pain. This opens the door to investigate mutually beneficial ideas.

Four key categories of business justification for sustainability include: operational efficiency, customer acquisition and growth, risk management, and employee engagement. Each of these has a direct, well-studied and documented tie to the financial bottom line. Here are questions to explore when seeking what will make executives perk up:

OPERATIONAL EFFICIENCY CATEGORY

- What is the energy usage trend for your business over the last few years? Is it moving up or down? What might factor into spikes of energy usage?

- What is the water usage trend for your business over the last few years? Is it moving up or down? What contributes to spikes in water usage?

- What major expenditures or projects on the horizon could be considered through the lens of sustainability? For example, are replacement or upgrades to HVAC, major appliances, windows, and fixtures scheduled?

- What minor and ongoing purchases could be considered through the lens of sustainability? For example, this is an opportunity to review the energy efficiency of light bulbs, batteries, small appliances, etc.

- How much waste do you generate each week/month/year? Do you have opportunities to increase the amount recycled or lower contamination rates of recycling?

- Have you reviewed your purchasing contracts to reduce packaging and shipping frequency, arrange for take-backs or other purchasing optimization?

CUSTOMER ACQUISITION CATEGORY

- What does your target audience think about sustainability? What issues matter most to them?

- What comments on review sites, or from customers, can be directly attributed to sustainability (or lack thereof)?

- What are your competitors doing in terms of sustainability? Are any of them eco-certified? Do they feature sustainability in their messaging?

- How do you capitalize on top trends in your sector?

- What features, products, or services related to sustainability would generate new revenue or augment existing products and services (for example, branded eco-merchandise or upsell for organic ingredients)?

RISK AND COMPLIANCE CATEGORY

- What elevated risks of flooding, drought, or other conditions could impact your organization's operations?

- In what ways do investors and creditors expect disclosure on sustainability performance?

- Does the business have an updated emergency plan? Have managers performed emergency drills and kept policies and procedures up-to-date?

- Have you trained and prepared employees to deal with human rights violations, such as harassment or sex trafficking?

- What is the organization's hazardous materials (for example paints or certain chemicals) policy?

- What local laws, or potential new policy, related to environmental, social, or governance issues might impact your business in the next twelve months?

EMPLOYEE ENGAGEMENT CATEGORY

- How has your company performed on the most recent engagement scores? What areas of weakness need to be addressed? What strengths can be optimized?

- What current corporate responsibility initiatives are employees actively engaged in? Do they ignore or pass on any? What have employees expressed interest in with regards to involvement and volunteerism?

- What is the turnover rate? How difficult is it to find employees with the right knowledge and skills for open positions? How do you compare with competitors in terms of benefits and opportunities for employees? What is your commitment or policy on diversity and inclusion?

- How often are employees trained? Do they have any special development or leadership opportunities?

Are employees trained on the company's social or environmental activities?

You can see right away the value of working as a team! If you have pulled together a cross-functional group (for example, green team), they can investigate these questions from the standpoint of different departments. A significant source of intel on what matters to executives lies in the next levels of leadership who report to them. They are a testing ground and practice audience as you prepare to take your ideas to the top.

EXPONENTIAL IMPACT APPLICATION AND DISCUSSION

- Work with your internal champions to answer questions listed in this chapter for determining the business case. Have at least one compelling idea with potential return and business benefits in each category.

- Check out Bob Willard's website Sustainability Advantage.[2] He offers free business case toolkits you can download and use to develop a business case. These are advanced tools with extensive Excel workbooks. Don't put pressure on yourself to be an expert. Start with the questions above and bookmark this tool for when you're ready to get more sophisticated with your business case proposal.

CHAPTER 6

DOWN: THE FRONT LINES OF IMPACT

THE STRATEGIC DISCONNECT

Don't mistake *"down"* as less than. This is purely a function of the way organizational charts visually appear on a page as well as common nomenclature around organizational structures such as *"lower level"* and *"upper level."* Based on my observations and the experiences of champions I've interviewed, some of those *"higher up"* do not appreciate the value or support the role of other levels of the organization.

IDEO put it perfectly. "For many organizations, frontline workers like grocery store clerks, nurses, hospitality workers, and transit employees are an essential part of doing business....As the point of contact with customers and key systems, these workers often know exactly when, where, and why things don't work, and they come up with powerful hacks and workarounds to make things better. Yet these insights and innovations rarely make it to the corporate office. And that's a problem: large organizations often hire design and innovation consulting firms while not taking advantage of a latent source of deep, in-house expertise. It's equally discouraging to workers who would gladly share their ideas if they were only asked."[1]

To practice empathy, I need the line levels' outlook on the issues at hand. I want to hear them grumble about the status quo and dream of a better tomorrow. I connect the dots between their input and the strategic direction of an overall sustainability program. Developing such a strategy is complex work, but the hardest part of my job is convincing executives to let me access the right levels.

One Gen Z champion I interviewed stated, "Those at the top, they're not seeing, they're not sharing with the people down below. That's the old world of top-down leadership. Executives see what needs to happen and tell them what to do. I feel that's shifting. People don't want that anymore."

Upper levels may see lower levels as cogs in a machine who have no care or place in strategic or altruistic initiatives. General managers and vice presidents have literally told me line-level staff *"only want a paycheck."* When executives assume people at the lower echelons are only there to punch a clock, they presuppose categorically staff are there to undercut, steal, and cause problems. Their words, not mine.

Similarly, I've lost count of the number of times my questions or recommendations are waved off with something like, *"Oh, that's the union,"* meaning *"we don't want to negotiate or take a stance with this powerful entity."* Unfortunately, just because union workers perform tasks related to sustainability doesn't mean you get a pass when it comes to reporting and accountability on their compliance.

Conversely, I have toured buildings where executives proudly pointed out a brilliant solution to a tough problem and gave direct credit to the worker, oftentimes a unionized employee, who came up with the idea. I wish I could say this was the rule, not the exception. The norm is indifference, but even that means line-level staff are overlooked as a resource in sustainability strategy.

Corporate leaders must focus on risks such as absenteeism, loss, workers' compensation claims, and productivity declines. They, therefore, fear the worst. This fosters an environment where employees do not feel compelled to give more of themselves than the bare minimum, if that.

This implies workers are uninterested in the upskilling required to effectively implement social and environmental programs. The *Voice of the American Workforce Survey Report*, which looks largely at line-level and hourly worker perspectives, reveals both money and advancement matter. For example, 67.2 percent of logistics workers indicated pay as the top quality in looking for a job and 66.8 percent claim pay tops the list for staying at their current job.[2] Upskilling and compensation are connected, as evidenced by the 67.3 percent who chose earning more pay as the top reason to learn a new skill.[3]

Money as a motivator to drive engagement is not a bad thing. Sustainability may be about helping society but that should never come at the expense of exploiting staff.

Once we get past pay rate, other factors are in play. About 20 percent on average indicated they left their last job due to lack of growth opportunities.[4] Other studies also uncover the importance of providing professional development. A 2021 study by WorkStep of more than 18,000 frontline workers across 150 companies showed the number one source of attrition was lack of career growth opportunities.[5]

For this reason, my primary apparatus for engaging this level of the organization is interactive workshops. I create space for listening and observing, preparing staff for what's to come, igniting passion, and generating momentum for change.

Sustainability champions trying to move the needle need to speak on the frontline level. Never to speak down but respect and accommodate the perspectives of others based not only on their personal interests but also their organizational context.

Most staff are just starting their sustainability journey, and some unwillingly. They don't necessarily grasp the magnitude or implications of sustainability or how their work or long-term career plays into that. Lower levels of the organization are not typically included in developing strategies, prioritizing initiatives, setting goals, or assigning resources, so they may be impatient about execution. They'll have a million ideas that are perfectly valid in their view but will not have framed them within the organization's boundaries. It's a delicate balancing act to hear them but also push back on what is feasible and best for the overall organization.

I encounter this in my work because I seek to connect with line cooks, banquet servers, stewards, and so forth. Their ideas for solving food waste problems are novel and oftentimes brilliant; however, they are not factoring in budgets, local waste infrastructure, regulations, and other barriers to perfectly good ideas. I focus on the positive and help them realize we must zoom out and look at this on a larger scale and see that over time progress can be accomplished, but it's not going to be perfect.

Staff do not always comprehend the concepts of span of control or scope. For example, I presented a sustainability strategy to staff at a client organization. Someone in the room expressed a desire to see that what they do changes how employees practice sustainability at home. While that is a virtuous desire, given where this organization is in its journey, this would not be a good use of time and energy.

On the one hand, this person's interest divulges a lot of insight. He is well-liked and has a positive influence on coworkers. I didn't want to squelch this idea, but on the other hand, I knew it was not going to be a strategic use of the team's very limited resources to go around trying to convince people to recycle at home, eat organic food, or buy an electric vehicle.

I knew it was inevitable their work would transform the general staff's lifestyle choices toward sustainability. I also recognized they were not yet in a position to discern or set strategic direction, so I met them where they were and walked them to the point of acknowledging why another focus would be better. Ideally this happens such that people are convinced without feeling ignored.

A powerful mechanism for receiving input from all levels and ensuring strategic and financial alignment with plans is to adopt an employee stock ownership plan (ESOP). You'll find an example of an ESOP company, Bob's Red Mill, maker of baking mixes and more, on the shelves of most grocery stores in the US. The founder, Bob Moore, tired of averting offers to buy his company and wanting to retain the mission-orientation of the business, converted to an ESOP in 2010 and reached one hundred percent employee ownership in 2020.[6]

I frequently harp on the lack of commitment to training and engaging the ranks at the bottom of organizational charts. This resistance is less prevalent in ESOPs. In a report from the Aspen Institute, ESOP employees received training at roughly double the rate of non-ESOP employees.[7] ESOP employees have greater access than their non-ESOP counterparts to actively participate in organizational development through mechanisms such as employee involvement teams.[8]

Furthermore, ESOPs are better at responding to global trends and crises. They employ Blacks, Latinos, and women at rates higher than their respective percentage of the population.[9] During COVID-19, ESOPs experienced a mean decline in employment of 4.8 percent while other firms saw a mean decrease of 19.5 percent.[10]

THE HEART DISCONNECT

The societal problems we're trying to solve are often far removed from our daily lives; however, it is the everyday life of some staff we ask to comply with sustainability policies. We ask them to care as if they are being benevolent because that's how we see ourselves in this work. But if you live surrounded by poverty, hunger, illiteracy, violence, flooding, and pollution, this all takes on a whole new meaning.

The front lines of the organization are literally on the front lines of our planetary and societal woes. Their quality of life is dependent on our ability to solve big, hairy problems. They draw the conclusion that their employer may contribute to the problem but do not necessarily see a connection to the solution.

I conducted training at a convention center where the leadership was able to get a room packed with lower levels of the organization. They ranged from those who sat in the front and took notes to those in the back of the room who seemed apathetic at best. The front rows were mostly women who had worked there for decades. They truly cared about their place of work. They were the heartbeat and backbone of the operation.

Those in the back rows sat as far from the point of engagement as possible. I learned through years of teaching college and training teams to just let it go sometimes. In a corporate setting, you do the best you can, and as long as it's not disruptive, you let it slide.

When I conduct training, it's collaborative, so everyone in the room is part of a small group at a flip chart throughout the day. I remember one guy who was distinctive because he had long dreadlocks and scowled at me all day. That's okay, I understood he may have forfeited a day off for this. He probably had been made to sit through a lot of awful and boring training. Maybe he'd had traumatic experiences in classrooms where he was belittled. He reluctantly participated in the training but others in the room more than made up for it with their enthusiasm.

See how easily empathy can border on stereotyping? It's hard to avoid, and profiling people is something we all do subconsciously so we must be careful. Given I was there only one day to train fifty people, it's hard for me to practice much personal empathy. I try through questions and creative tasks. Still, I am exposed mostly to the surface, and my own unconscious bias fills in the blanks. Those who run the organization don't have the excuse of limited exposure. They have plenty of opportunity to empathize and learn about their staff.

A few months later, I was back at that convention center to attend a conference. Staff approached me and asked, "Do you remember Donald? The guy with dreads." She continued, "He came in a few days after the training and said he noticed a donation truck in his neighborhood, and he started asking about our donation program."

As he and others start to notice, connect the dots, mention their observations, and participate in programs, the needle moves. It may be almost imperceptible at times but in the hearts and minds of these staff members, this deepens their connection to the organization, to their teammates, to their community, and likely even to their own success and well-being.

Minorities in an organization may have even greater connections to initiatives. Research from WeSpire on employee engagement in sustainability initiatives showed people of color were 45 percent more likely to rate impact programs as very or extremely effective than their white peers.[11] This same study showed people of color had a highly unmet desire for diversity, equity, and inclusion (DEI) programs in their places of work.

It is critical to fill these gaps. In the WeSpire study, 19 percent of all respondents claimed no sustainability programs were offered that matched their area of passion.[12] This is untapped potential to generate exponential impact.

Listening to the heartbeat of staff helps us avoid being on the wrong side of issues when they arise. Don't get me wrong, I'm not so naive as to think a perfectly clear right and wrong exists for every issue. Solutions can be too nuanced for staff to fully appreciate, but that doesn't mean they shouldn't be asked what's the most effective strategy to combat racism or climate change.

Clearly these are complex issues, so it's not as much about a definitive position as it is about studying and evolving. Thoughtfully communicate where you are on the journey and, more importantly, your willingness to change position as the research and insights demand. If your programs do not connect with the interests of staff, employees are not likely to go the extra mile to volunteer, learn new skills, or change behavior, much less lead others to do the same.

Think about it. If you give someone the bare minimum of your heart, they're going to give you the bare minimum of theirs. Social and environmental initiatives are increasingly strategic rather than just philanthropic, but don't forget the power of emotions at play when it comes to the ills we face and hope to solve.

EXPONENTIAL IMPACT APPLICATION AND DISCUSSION

- What aspects of existing or planned sustainability programs are most dependent on the buy-in of the organization's front line? What are potential challenges and opportunities in engaging them in the design and planning elements of initiatives?

- What do you perceive as barriers between upper and lower levels of your organization? If you are fortunate enough to be where the top and bottom of the organization are well-connected, how would you characterize what is going well?

- What existing instruments could be leveraged for soliciting input from the line level of your organization (as it relates to social and environmental issues)? Are there questionnaires or listening forums? Training sessions? Social occasions?

CHAPTER 7

AROUND: ORGANIZATIONAL CULTURE

OLD DOGS, NEW TRICKS

Imagine you're a contestant on a reality show and you're dropped somewhere unfamiliar. You're assigned an objective but don't even know where to start. What is the terrain? What will you eat? How will you find your way to safety? I can't imagine doing this, much less naked!

Walking into a new organizational context, right in the middle of major projects or change, is like being thrown into an unknown wilderness. When sustainability is in the mix, added complexity increases the difficulty level of the task. This unknown wilderness you face is the tricky nature of the organization's culture.

"Around," or culture, refers to the interdepartmental and interpersonal nature of an organization and the

effectiveness of communication and engagement or, more likely, the lack thereof. Gallup conducts an annual survey of employee engagement, an indicator for the health of an organization's culture. The 2023 results (reflecting 2022 data) showed engagement levels have declined in recent years to 32 percent and the ratio of engaged to disengaged employees is 1.8 to 1, the lowest in almost a decade.[1]

What drives this point home is Gallup's description of these respective categories—engaged employees are "involved in and enthusiastic about their work and their workplace" while disengaged employees are "disgruntled and disloyal."[2] If nearly one fifth of your workforce were practically sabotaging your business, seems like something you'd want to address!

Nothing exposes how bad the culture is like sustainability initiatives. The organization's history creates almost invisible barriers, but these are obstacles nonetheless. Divisions between departments construct the infamous silos that prevent the flow of communication. Riffs between people run so deep and long no one remembers what started the feud in the first place. Old-timers established unwritten rules that show up as "we've just always done it this way."

My favorite example of this came from food waste training with a hotel catering team. I explained that of the prolifically problematic items we waste in events, fruit platters are among the worst offenders. Specifically, honeydew and cantaloupe are tossed out more often.

A captain in the room, with a tenure of more than twenty years at that hotel, piped up. "But melon is cheap."

I responded, "Congratulations. You didn't pay much for that trash."

It was like a bomb went off. They reeled from this sudden, startling realization. Many years ago, a few people in the industry must have decided it was better to have fruit go into the trash than risk showing a bare spot on a platter.

This is how habits have literally become institutionalized. Staff who have been around a long time have a tight grip on these notions. Their pride and dignity are on the line if you disagree with their assumptions.

Enter a new employee raring to go.

Ilena was that person in a sports arena undergoing renovations. Amid a large and complex operation, a new person waltzed in ready to help, but no one wanted to dance. Buildings like this are typically publicly owned (by the city or county) with a lot of opiniated stakeholders. Ilena explained, "Some people have been here twenty, thirty, forty years. When I get in there, I don't want to be the know-it-all, but at the same time, I'm watching department heads do things I had to do by myself for ten years at my old job."

It's tempting to feel a newcomer has nothing valuable to offer and, on the flip side, young professionals might discount the wisdom that comes with being on a job for a long time. In my experience, sustainability champions are more likely to be greenhorns, so their ideas may be dismissed. Coworkers may be skeptical, maybe even threatened by this new, eager energy. When it comes right down to it, people just don't take well to change.

Pushing sustainability in an organization necessitates modifying routines. The champions are comfortable with it, but they face inertia that cannot be understated. Personally, I thrive on change! I have moved an average of every three years since I was eighteen. I've worked in five different industries in a dozen various functions. Some people, though, settle into a familiar regimen and have no interest in budging. When a group of people in an organization go for so long without any significant adjustments, they atrophy.

How people do their jobs unofficially or *"off the books"* also factors into how sustainability initiatives play out. Workarounds can be messy to unravel, habits hard to break. A conversation focused on technical details only gets you so far. Discovering the real problem requires insight and discernment about elements you can't easily see on the surface.

An outsider may see this more clearly. Ilena did, but she recognized how challenging it is to get people to change. "All these city partners knew I'd done this work previously. They figured I would have set these folks straight, but it was hard to convince people who'd been there so long. The city partners are looking at me like, 'What is wrong with these people?' The team in this building had operated like an island for so long and then got this infusion of resources and outside partners, who wanna tell them to jump and expect them to say, 'How high?' It doesn't work like that."

Waste management exposes these issues rather starkly. Trash talk can literally lead to trash talk! Waste solutions are not one-size-fits-all and are ridiculously complicated. When I train on this topic, I attempt to engage staff in designing new solutions to increase diversion from landfill; however, I first have to get through the grumbling and finger-pointing about the general state of recycling in the building.

A customary design for waste management is to color code bins—such as blue for recycling, green for compost, black for landfill. If the same color bags are in all three bins, what happens by the time all of these make their way to the dock? What's the likelihood waste ends up in its designated stream? How does it make people feel when someone puts the right item in the right bin but someone else negates the effort by not doing their part?

I once observed a line cook slicing ends and tops off fennel and tossing them in a trash bin along with plastic wrap, cardboard, and other trash. Never mind that those fennel pieces could have been repurposed into other items (sauces, garnishes, etc.) and this kitchen had a compost program.

The compost bin was about three feet away on the other side of a stack of trays from where the cook was prepping.

The bags in both bins were black; however, the bin colors were different. From the top, though, all I could see was a black bag pulled over the top rim of a bin. If, out of convenience, the cook grabbed what's closest to him, who knows what we'd end up with? Before this, no one noticed much, but once they became aware, it was easy to quickly jump to judgment.

At another building, clear bags were preferred for recycling because it allowed staff to police each other on whether materials were going into proper bags. While this can still cause confusion, it highlights something about the accepted dynamic among staff when they can call each other out for not complying correctly with recycling standards.

One problem or decision area will prompt a change across the board. Watch for ripple-effect decisions where a choice to change something in one area will have unforeseen consequences in another. If those people were not included or considered, they could dodge the effort or interfere with the intention. I witnessed this in the hotel industry when green cleaning products were introduced. Housekeeping staff were not part of the decisions and rebelled. Some even brought in cleaning products from home! They also misused the new, green options, which rendered the cleaning agents ineffective and perpetuated the myth that green cleaning doesn't work.

Of the barriers preventing sustainability initiatives from moving forward, organizational silos are the most important to address. These may exist along departmental lines or be based on the physical layout of a building. Internal planning, training, operations, and communication happen within these silos. An absence of empathy for and understanding of what others contribute to the organization's mission prevents effective program implementation.

CLOSING THE GAP

The culture described above makes empathy difficult to exercise. How do you decipher and read between the lines to move efforts forward? How do you dismantle departmental discord to get people to a place where they share and collaborate? How much more difficult is this via email and video conferencing?

That's just to execute the simplest of initiatives. The greater the ambition, the more critical the connections and interactions. You'd be amazed how much you can accomplish and how many objections you can overcome once you get people communicating and cooperating.

> *"You'd be amazed how much you can accomplish and how many objections you can overcome once you get people communicating and cooperating."*

For example, many organizations are setting zero waste targets. Achieving such a lofty target requires teams across an organization to determine ways to innovate input materials, reduce production by-products, and improve recycling systems. Product designers, plant managers, janitorial services, and other departments must have a say-so in the solutions, which are often complex and heretofore unknown. Each department tends to think their need should override that of others. Whether it's budget, physical layouts, time, or other resources, everyone is going to have an opinion and a priority.

Henkel, manufacturer of recognizable home and laundry products, has a zero-waste objective that it is reaching through not only cross-functional teamwork, but also among locations around the US.[3] One location partnered with another in a different state and found waste from one plant could be used as an input in the other.[4] These solutions not only reduced waste, they even created a new revenue stream! One plant addressed a problem stemming from changing out colors in a manufacturing process. Rather than throwing out the sealant, they can now sell a blended, off-colored product for applications where color is not a factor.[5]

The most constructive mechanism for reaching staff throughout an organization is a cross-functional sustainability task force (often known as a green team). They typically meet monthly for an hour, and through discussions about sustainability topics, a greater view into the overall organization emerges. Members learn about people and processes they never knew about. Empathy happens whether you intended it or not.

Green teams are especially advantageous in larger, dispersed organizations, but even small businesses can benefit from the open lines of communication they foster. Ideally, a green team consists of representatives from every department, but don't let perfect get in the way of good. If you only find one other person willing to join you for regular meetings, start there!

I consider green teams so important that you will see the concept intertwined in many chapters of this book. They are vital when organizations are starting their sustainability journey because no official responsibility exists for it. If it's no one's job, it's no one's job. In the early stages, a green team is the interim sustainability department. Later, when a sustainability department officially exists, the green team serves as a conduit for communication and implementation of social and environmental initiatives.

Green teams only reach so far and are a space and time entity with sporadic and short meetings. To take the organizational integration and empathy to the next level, employ job shadowing. You reach those outside the green team, and it's a more specific and focused arrangement that creates strong cross-functional cohesion.

A champion I interviewed began his sustainability role in a foodservice chain in job shadow mode. "The last year was a lot about integration and being among staff in different departments. I had to do a lot of listening on my end just to see where everyone was and how open everyone was to incorporate my ideas." Spending time learning about those tasked to carry out the mission was a brilliant way to develop empathy and build relationships crucial to driving lasting change.

A benefit of job shadowing across departments is identifying the path of least resistance for your ideas. Select the tier two champions who would be willing to pilot ideas. Leverage their openness to create solid programs that can later be rolled out to hundreds or thousands of employees.

Like showing executives the business case covered in an earlier chapter, staff will be grateful for the operational efficiencies. I hear this after I come in and train on preventing waste. They later comment they see the difference, and it makes their job easier. That can be a happy accident, or you can proactively inquire about the details of their work processes. This frame of reference makes a notable difference in both the effectiveness of and the receptiveness to the changes you recommend.

EXPONENTIAL IMPACT APPLICATION AND DISCUSSION

As a sustainability champion or green team, anticipate pushback from coworkers and staff. I offer a technique for working through objections: Write mock emails from staff, pretending to be in their frame of mind and rejecting an invitation to serve on the green team or participate in a sustainability program.

This exercise is incredibly enlightening. Without my prompting, clients often take an almost extreme approach to how coworkers might respond to such requests. This gives them a worst-case scenario viewpoint. They know their coworkers, so a particularly vocal opposer is often the prototype.

Even if you do not have a fully formed or active green team, band together with like-minded champions and try this exercise. Work through your defensiveness and eye-rolling so you can facilitate productive interactions.

Here are samples of rejection emails I've kept over the years:

Sample #1:

Dear Green Team Organizer,

I appreciate your interest in selecting me. However, I can't picture this company running a successful green team. I highly doubt the company would take this matter seriously, and it'll turn into a complete mess with the lack of funds and assistance.

Since this is a volunteer act, most people are not willing to pick up the extra work without being paid for it, so how would we even be able to progress without the right number of people, nevertheless with a positive mindset?

How can we get others to believe the importance of sustainability with such little information about the outcomes for both the team and company? I see your effort in trying to explain this the best way you can, but how would we all benefit from this? Don't get me wrong, this may be a great idea, but I don't think it'll be the best for the company as of right now, especially with all that's been happening with our world. It's already hard enough to get anyone's attention so what makes you think anyone would want to spend more time working without getting paid and being tired after a long day?

We need to find better ways to reward our team and keep them engaged; otherwise, meetings will be pointless and a waste of time. Let's focus on managing the company first and then consider this down the road.

Thank you for reaching out and I hope we can do this the right way.

Best Regards,
Alex

Take a moment to consider the concerns:

- The company will lack follow-through, as it seems it may have done with other initiatives. It sounds like projects tend to be underfunded and unsupported. This is a recurring theme in most of the examples I've read, which shows me even members of the green team have their doubts about the organization's true commitment.

- It's a burden for staff without a corresponding reward, particularly in the form of money. This also comes up in almost every rejection email I've seen.

- They are reacting to what might be a vague call to action. They want more details. This is another recurring theme, showing green teams struggle with the language and specificity of sustainability.

Sample #2:

Dear Green Team Captain,

Thank you for presenting your ideas for the green team to me and my colleagues yesterday. While I did find most of your ideas rather interesting, I am not entirely convinced the development of a green team within this organization is truly necessary. This initiative sounds attractive in theory, but I do not believe it will develop the way you might envision it. Employees, investors, and customers may seem excited and motivated at first, but it will likely become very old very quickly.

I hate to sound so negative, but I am speaking from experience. The company attempted a green team a few years ago, and it was mostly a disaster. There was very little leadership or sense of direction. Everyone seemed to have brilliant ideas, but whenever it came time to execute, there was no action. We initially scheduled biweekly meetings, which eventually became monthly meetings, then quarterly meetings, then no meetings at all. Then just like that, there was no more green team.

The company has quite a few green policies in place, like a two-sided printing policy and mandatory shutdown of machines at the end of each day. With those two policies alone, the company is doing its part. I do not know if a green team can reduce our carbon footprint any further.

I trust you will find members within this organization who share your passion and optimism. I wish you all the best with the development of this team!

Regards,
Anne

Let's evaluate the concerns expressed here:

- Once again, we see she has doubts the company can follow through on its commitments.

- Of note here is that Anne was part of a defunct green team. She might feel unappreciated and frustrated her efforts were not as meaningful as she'd hoped they would be.

- She has a limited view of sustainability. This is another common thread in the emails. Staff feel recycling or basic initiatives are pretty much the full list of possibilities. Alternatively, they think "this is all great, but what about the issue I care about." As noted earlier, it's useful to familiarize yourself with coworkers' social and environmental priorities.

You may face resistance based on employees' stance on social, environmental, and political issues; however, it is their nebulous attitudes about the organization and their coworkers that create hidden barriers a change agent must overcome. Confronting this head-on allows you to ascertain more quickly the nature of the concerns and whether they're easily addressed or require more finesse. Equally important to the role-play putting yourself in others' shoes is the follow-on exercise where you prepare empathetic responses to these emails. This pairs well with the earlier chapter encouraging you to know your own hidden motivations.

CHAPTER 8

ACROSS: STRENGTH IN NUMBERS

BUILDING BRIDGES

In one of my favorite sports-themed movies, two enemies within the same team come together to beat bigger enemies—the opposing team and the racism that pervaded their community. I love stories of unlikely pairs banding together for a greater cause. Inevitably, they must lay aside conflict and competition, even if temporarily, to achieve a common goal.

Earlier, I covered the power of relationships with community partners who can help you empathize with stakeholders more in their realm of familiarity than yours. Now, let's expand the concept to include partnerships forged within your organization's network of clients, vendors, and competitors. Here, empathy is extended to the overall ecosystem within which you operate and the way you can, together, reap the benefits of exponential impact.

The dynamic is more contentious by default. When dealing with clients or vendors, a natural power struggle results in favorable (or unfavorable) terms and conditions. Even when the business relationship is symbiotic, everyone has their own way of doing things and expectations clash. Of course, competitors are natural enemies as you each fight for the same customers and investors. Likewise in the government or nonprofit world, each agency must compete for limited funding and resources.

When it comes to social and environmental impact, you are likely to have more in common with clients, vendors, and competitors than not. Ideally, you come together with common sustainability goals, but even better is when the success of each is inextricably linked to others. An example of this going well is the initiative Chance led to certify five organizations to one set of industry standards.

In the trade show and conference industry, the ecosystem consists of destinations (destination management or marketing organizations, or convention and visitors bureaus), convention centers, caterers, audiovisual producers and technicians, and other service providers. Typically, a different vendor oversees each of these. Chance worked in one of those organizations, and as sustainability was gaining traction among event organizers, he seized the opportunity to differentiate not just his employer, but the entire ecosystem in his city.

I've known Chance several years, and when he goes for something, he shoots for the moon! Like me, he's an extreme optimist and comes up with audacious ideas.

(One of my clients kids me and says I'm in a Xanadu state with some of my proposals.) Chance's accomplishment fortifies my hope that radical schemes are possible.

Chance proposed multiple organizations work together for their respective certifications. These entities were interlinked from a business perspective anyway, and together they could achieve exponential impact.

Chance attributed this feat to collaboration. "The buy-in from leadership was strong from the start. We put together a green team with about thirty founding members across five organizations. You had general managers, housekeepers, and everything in between. And we got the certifications! We didn't know it, but it was the first time it had been done in the industry as a shared partnership. We got a lot of recognition, which was great for the destination. It was really successful."

When organizations are so interconnected, it's inevitable challenges emerge among them as the flow of work and communication from one to the next can be hindered by misunderstandings, bureaucracy, and lack of resources. Each feels their needs are the highest priority, their problems are the most difficult. The collective learns more about what each organization struggles with in the effort to make a positive impact and this empathy enables more cooperation in identifying common pathways forward.

For projects like this to work, forging relationships within a community ecosystem is an integral part of success. This was demonstrated well by one restaurant group that was expanding and sought sustainability services to scale with them. This required a significant commitment because they were in an area with insufficient composting infrastructure to support their needs. For most restaurant owners, that would be the end of the conversation. Composting would move to the back burner until the local infrastructure caught up. When sustainability is viewed as optional and the way is not smooth or obvious, leaders go a different direction, taking the path of least resistance.

But not this dedicated team. They spent four years researching, outreaching, exploring, and partnering. Ultimately, they chose to help a compost company expand operations so the composter could handle the restaurant group's needs. This goes beyond just one company taking an order from another and flipping on the service. This took many detailed operational conversations to figure out what would work and what wouldn't. It took running pilots or tests in a cooperative manner where success was equally tied to both parties. One restaurateur's willingness to be a trailblazer enabled the composter to service other restaurants competing on the merits of sustainability. This act expanded the pie from which the whole local hospitality community could feast.

Partnership means your needs and theirs are more deeply intertwined. Empathetic listening can take you far when it comes to setting a mission, strategy, priorities, and implementation plans, but when it comes to partnership, listening isn't enough. The two-way nature of this relationship means empathy entails negotiation, compromise, dialogue, and alignment. That's how it becomes exponential.

"Partnership means your needs and theirs are more deeply intertwined."

While partnerships might be forged and formalized at the highest levels of organizations, it's the operational staff and middle management who will carry it through and be required to communicate and track progress with their counterparts in partner organizations. Their concerns will be less strategic and more tactical and transactional in nature. Partnerships may be formed for the splash, but success depends on all parties being saturated in the purpose and each doing their part.

Valerie shared a tactic that helped her successfully navigate this dynamic. She implements sustainability for large events with dozens of exhibitors and vendors. In this multifaceted scenario, she employed empathy to get consent. "I understand everybody's swamped and worried about their own thing. It took time for me to realize my thing is not their thing. And the way they see it, my thing is essentially taking away from them being able to do their thing. Now my approach is to first seek to understand what it is they do and what their pain points are, what matters to them, what is a relief to them, and then focus on those things so they get it, in a communication method that resonates with how they regularly operate."

Good leadership and partnership mean balancing overlapping and competing priorities. Imagine a scenario where a mall management company wants to install sustainability expectations and policies for tenants. What if some of the retailers have contradictory corporate policies?

For example, perhaps the mall management noticed how much paper gets tossed into the recycle bin as well as the garbage, so they decided to contract with a shredding service to pick up from all the mall's stores. The local shredding company may insist on an exclusivity deal in exchange for an excellent rate. What if a store in the mall is part of a national retail chain with its own exclusive contract with a different shredding service who has already been picking up from that store? Now the staff in this store may feel their efforts weren't noticed or appreciated by mall management who didn't even consult them on this plan. A lack of empathy for the context early on in these situations creates headaches and expense down the road.

Collaboration with third parties strengthens the business case for sustainability. This is how Diana built a solid case for a major sustainability investment at a large hotel in New York City. As she was introducing sustainability initiatives, she boldly reached out to competitors for help. She wanted to install composting machines in three kitchens, and this took some convincing because it meant other equipment would have to be moved and someone's job would go from taking garbage from point A to point B, to now separating and handling food waste in a new way. Diana needed hard evidence this would work.

She went the extra mile to collect compelling information from vendors and competitors. "I asked for numbers on the reduction of garbage bags. I asked how others worked with the union to change the responsibilities for staff. How did they get these machines into the hotels? How did they do preventive maintenance? I actually went to the other hotels and asked for a walkthrough. I took pictures and videos so when I went to our general manager and owners, we were ready to answer questions related to operations, engineering, cost, maintenance, and union management."

The notion of working with competitors to achieve social and environmental impact is tough for some to swallow. Of importance to executives is a focus on accelerating growth and market share, protecting intellectual property, and keeping a tight lid on internal processes and data. Still, they seek positive impact (whether spurred by regulations, investors, or customers), and a precompetitive approach is necessary to see shifts in how the entire industry operates.

THE TIDE RAISES ALL BOATS

Sustainability creates opportunities for discussions and sharing of ideas and best practices among competitors. Everyone gives lip service to the idea of coming together to solve the big problems, but when it gets down to it, it's herding cats and pulling teeth. Those in an industry may acknowledge the big hairy problems in their sector, but admitting it is risky. This equates to accepting responsibility for outcomes many executives still do not believe they should own.

This situation needs an umpire, someone who can mediate the work required to drive industry or community-wide impact. Nonprofits are an excellent conduit for this. They are a neutral third party and their goal is social or environmental impact, not market share or profits. The 2023 *Edelman Trust Barometer* shows forces that divide and forces that unify—business leaders, nonprofits, and teachers—were the only organizations seen to be more unifying than divisive.[1]

Nonprofits, industry associations, and government agencies can create a safe space where industry players collaborate in a precompetitive manner and sometimes also with clients. They form committees tasked to address critical problems plaguing the entire industry or supply chain. They offer resources, such as training, technology, or advocacy when perhaps the industry is not yet willing.

These agreements and working groups tend to be driven by and consist of corporate-level leaders. High level, strategic decision makers convene, point out problems and solutions, and make a pledge to change. I've seen such efforts fail. I won't name them here as they don't deserve chastisement. This stuff is hard!

As noted already, the missing link in these setups is the inclusion of those who will carry the torch. At the risk of being repetitive, I can't emphasize this enough. We ultimately need staff on the ground buying in and driving change. Even when solutions are technological and system driven, you'd be amazed how easy it is for a human to intervene and circumvent intended outcomes.

Getting corporate executives on a call is challenging enough, but getting store, property, factory, and line-level staff involved is next-level difficult. A lack of interest does not stand in the way; it's managements' resistance to making staff available for training and meetings. I'll cover the trials and tribulations of getting the right levels trained in the Enlighten Section.

A case study in the challenges and successes of such endeavors is the Pacific Coast Food Waste Commitment (PCFWC), a cooperation among the governments of California, Oregon, Washington, and British Columbia to achieve key sustainability targets, including cutting food waste in half by 2030. PCFWC's initiatives have brought together various members of food-related industries. They formed working groups and funded pilots to address problematic areas of food waste.

I led pilot projects for PCFWC in the hospitality industry, working with hotels and convention centers on food waste prevention. Participants hailed from two hotel brands and two venue catering companies. I sincerely hoped to get the teams at the various locations on calls to discuss challenges and spread best practices. Staff were interested. Some even said, "It would be great if we could speak with other properties and learn what they're doing and share what we've learned." They were referring to properties under the same brand! If that's not working out well, what hope do we have in connecting banquet and culinary staff across different locations *and* brands?

The implications of partnerships should trickle down. I was aiming for that. I focused on engaging frontline hotel and convention center teams, which was quite successful, but on the other end, the higher-level, cross-property partnership was not as strong. In the story shared earlier, Chance discovered this truth and actively worked to create that cross-organization connection at both the higher and line levels.

PCFWC has successfully brought together partners in other segments of foodservice, food manufacturing, and grocery. This cross-sector empathy exposes common challenges and innovative solutions. You can read more about the hospitality pilots and other PCFWC projects at their website.[2]

Ultimately, we need to view partnerships as *"the whole is greater than the sum of the parts."* We tend to just see parts, particularly our part. The possibility of partnerships is exponential impact. We must lean into the time-consuming and complex nature of pulling these together and ideally do a better job integrating on-the-ground operational teams to carry out the mission of these powerful alliances.

EXPONENTIAL IMPACT APPLICATION AND DISCUSSION

- What type of organization outside your normal realm of partnership could help you achieve exponential impact? Which organizations in your ecosystem could fill gaps in your organization's capacity to achieve sustainability goals? (Or even get sustainability off the ground if that's the stage you're in.) Your ecosystem includes customers, vendors, industry associations, and other existing partners. For each category, identify where you can listen and share to find common ground.

- Research industry associations, working groups, and committees you can plug into.

- Which organizational leaders or employees do you immediately think of as the ones who should be responsible for outreach and establishing these partnerships?

- Now, challenge yourself to identify staff who would not normally be at this table but whose input could add insight and help champion an idea among their peers.

CHAPTER 9

ACROSS: AN EXTENSION OF THE FAMILY

WORKING WITH CONSULTANTS

My goal when working with clients is to work myself out of a job.

What? Yes, if I do my job well, I will expand their capacity to solve problems for which they initially hired me to decipher. Sure, I might still work with them on bigger, messier problems, but I don't want to be a crutch for everyday, ongoing tasks such as measurement, tracking, and reporting.

The lack of experience and talent to satisfy the growth in organizational sustainability roles means consultants may be necessary to fill the gap. Sustainability related degree and certificate options are popping up all over the place, but entry-level staff coming out of these programs are not likely to yet have the full breadth and depth of knowledge and expertise required for some priority initiatives.

In GreenBiz's 2022 *State of the Profession*, the Weinreb Group shared research on adding staffing or consultants because of increased pressure related to disclosures on performance and impact related to environmental, social, and governance (ESG) activities. Twenty percent of surveyed organizations have added one full-time employee, 30 percent have added more than one, and 35 percent indicated they have hired more consultants.[1]

These new positions are largely focused on reporting and storytelling. While more reflective of what has already taken place, these roles still require empathy and context to ensure accurate and authentic coverage. We can imagine an increase in reporting naturally reflects an increase in consultants for project design and implementation as well as an increase in staffing allocated to initiatives.

Advisers are sought after for their technical knowledge, and a sustainability specialist brings a wealth of information about solutions, timing, and methods required. Warning though: they may copy and paste solutions, skipping the empathy step. Without context, their rubber-stamped changes could end up rejected wholesale by staff.

Ilena, whom we already met, shared an example demonstrating how wrong consultants can get it. Before she stepped into the stadium renovation described earlier, she began her foray into sustainability helping staff in the administrative offices of an arena. Sustainability was introduced starting with basic initiatives like recycling. "This specialist came in and deployed a recycle bin at every desk. This consultant also decided it would be wise to remove the trash cans at every desk and only allow trash to be thrown out in pantries and kitchens. You would've thought the consultant had killed a thousand puppies. I mean it was, 'Oh my God, where's my trash can? What are we supposed to do? This is crazy!' Our executive director's assistant went bonkers and made the consultant cry."

Ilena dug deeper and realized there had never been a conversation with anyone in the C-suite nor their assistants. Someone applied a blanket solution and overlooked stakeholders to the detriment of the program. "It taught me you have to obtain buy-in. Everybody has to be on the same page. Everybody produces trash, and it has to go somewhere."

As a consultant, in a sense, I am a short-term employee of my client's organization. I see what I want to see, or only what is visible, and when I lack empathy, or exposure to the full story, it diminishes my effectiveness. I've learned, empathized, and therefore can identify where initiatives are likely to trip up, but I can only achieve that when I'm welcomed into the fold.

Stakeholder engagement is paramount to successful sustainability; however, I've worked with clients who want to bypass this phase. They do not grant access to staff or directors. This results in questionable deliverables and outcomes because I couldn't get the input needed for the best solution and because the plan's results are unknown. The scope of work ends, the contract expires, and I'm not sure how things turned out. Did they implement our ideas? Are they measuring what we recommended they track? Is the green team still meeting regularly?

I am denied the opportunity to learn and improve how my team performs. This is not a master plan clients have to exclude or block us. Rather, this behavior stems from dealing with an unknown topic while managing dozens of other priorities competing for attention and resources. Crises and control issues also thwart stakeholder access.

As a consultant, I must have empathy for all the angles covered in the Empathize section of this book. I naturally care about social and environmental causes, or I wouldn't be doing this work. I need to listen to outside stakeholders. I have to convince executives to pay my fees and assign the tasks. I must deliver compelling content and rally the front lines to add sustainability to their daily grind. I go in blind to an unfamiliar culture. When you add barriers to reaching those stakeholders, the work gets infinitely more challenging.

When both the consultant and the internal champion appreciate the needs and goals of the other, the work becomes more collaborative, more efficient, and more satisfying. Best practices for working with consultants and outsiders include the following:

- Enable relationship building. Empathy is difficult to achieve when there is no relationship. Consultants need direct access to the right stakeholders. It's common for a project to launch with no clear list of who is involved or how to best reach them. This means one person, such as an executive sponsor, is the filter, and they become a bottleneck. Furthermore, all ideas and opinions get interpreted by this one person who will have their own preference and agenda.

- Build empathy into the budget and timeline. If the scope of work includes opportunities to listen to and learn end user and decision maker needs, this takes time and resources. It also requires meeting space, marketing and communication efforts, incentives to draw in stakeholders, hours for planning and analysis, and participation by managers and staff.

- Don't completely outsource stakeholder engagement. On the one hand, we are treated like outsiders, and on the other, we become a proxy for the organization in key stakeholder interactions. This disconnect causes confusion because consultants cannot address some questions due to a lack of context or authority. If no internal representative is present, no opportunity for clarification or reinforcement will be available.

- Explain nuances of the organization's culture. Corporate values, interpersonal dynamics, departmental silos, and recent trauma (for example, layoffs, mergers) add color to the employee experience and input. Describe unspoken needs, assumptions, and challenges an outsider would not necessarily pick up on.

- Give the relevant industry context. A consultant may or may not be versed specifically in your sector. They may be experts in water or air quality, or waste-reduction technology, but not understand the latest crisis or trend driving the mentality or fear of those you need to convince or manage. Provide research and data whenever possible as this helps the consultant approach the input more objectively and better utilize it in problem solving.

Consultants benefit greatly from a *"walk a mile in someone else's shoes"* experience with their clients. Donna worked in a distribution center. The organization generated many types of waste, and the recycling setup was confusing with different containers and stacks for different types of waste. Donna and her colleagues are not specialists, so they were always putting the wrong materials in the wrong piles. Then the waste hauler would reject the pickup load or fine them for contamination. They were desperate for a better way of handling these materials and feeling the pressure from headquarters to meet corporate-wide sustainability goals.

Donna brought in someone to advise on waste solutions in the loading docks. This consultant's scope of work included ample time to learn context. He figured out waste handling would be greatly facilitated by marking indicators on the floors in addition to on the walls. Maintenance staff could only see the floor when moving waste from one area to another so what better spot to provide direction and instruction? This type of signage may be broadly applicable, but until you've walked the dock alongside staff, experiencing the solution as they do, listening to their remarks, reading their body language, you won't know for sure.

In this case, Donna worked side-by-side with the consultant, which created continuity because eventually the consultant goes away and someone needs to have intimate knowledge of how the solution is supposed to work. Organizations should have a succession plan for consultants, especially those significantly embedded in operations. I believe a good consultant works themselves out of a job with each client, but this is only possible when a level of empathy and connection is afforded from both sides.

EXPONENTIAL IMPACT APPLICATION AND DISCUSSION

- In what ways has your organization successfully worked with outside consultants? What have been criticisms or challenges in past consultant relationships? Were they afforded access to the staff and resources they needed to be effective?

- Which current social or environmental initiatives need the strategic or scientific support of a subject matter expert? How do you plan to identify and work with advisers for those initiatives?

- Prepare an organizational dossier you can share with any outside specialist so they are quickly acclimated to the dynamics. Include contacts of key players and when, why, and how they should be engaged in the scope of work at hand. Share backstories, policies, and other context critical to the success of the consultant's tenure with your organization.

PART 2:

ENLIGHTEN

CHAPTER 10

ENLIGHTEN: PRECURSOR TO IMPACT

BECAUSE I SAID SO

I hate *"because I said so."* You can imagine what a delight that was for my parents and teachers. It extends to bosses. Too many have a *"because I said so"* approach to leadership. I need to understand *why* you want me to do something. If I don't have the context or purpose, the work is boring and joyless.

Sustainability programs, like other corporate mandates, are rolled out with the *"because I said so"* method, leaving people who are supposed to do the work not understanding why. It's all the inconvenience and pain of change with none of the payoff.

Research shows this mentality in rolling out initiatives can be perceived as disrespectful. In the *Voice of the American Workforce Survey Report,* when asked what promotes employee loyalty, aside from salary, the top answer was "treat me with respect" which included "explaining workplace policies and rules."[1]

Sustainability spawns new policies, procedures, and controls. How these are explained is a critical and, in my experience, often neglected element of implementation. I review sustainability policies for clients. Given my background, I can fill in blanks left by baffling and incomplete instructions. However, staff will be confused and might ignore the policy rather than take time to figure out what their employer could have more clearly articulated.

The *"start with why"* concept has caught on in the corporate world (thank you, Simon Sinek), but it's still mainly happening in rooms where strategy is determined. Those at the top are not always good stewards of the *"why"*. They get it, so that feels like enough, and line-level staff are discounted as viable and valuable contributors in driving change.

This disconnect is not a new phenomenon, but sustainability shines a light on it because it often falls outside the realm of current job requirements. Even when it is compulsory, the quality of the work suffers when people don't connect with the purpose.

Increasingly, the *"why"* is social and environmental impact tied to the corporate mission and business model. Whether penetrating the upper ranks to change perspective and priorities or explaining initiatives to the line-level staff carrying out the operational implementation, getting buy-in is everything.

> *"Commitment rather than compliance!*
> *Now that's buy-in!"*

After conducting training at a convention center, I followed up to ask the executives what the biggest takeaway had been. The Director of Catering Operations shared his amazement to see line-level personnel experience "a sense of belonging." He elaborated, "Normally when new ideas are rolled out, the staff think it's just to save the company money, but this time, I saw commitment rather than compliance." Commitment rather than compliance! Now that's buy-in!

RAISING AWARENESS

Getting buy-in involves sparking interest, piquing curiosity, grabbing attention, and generating passion. Expecting people to have passion might be a stretch, but it does happen. Don't expect everyone in the organization to have the same zeal for the issue you have. If you just get as far as interest or curiosity with most people, you're ahead of the game!

Most sustainability professionals I interviewed said awareness is the priority engagement principle of the four I present in this book. They recognize the power in making the workforce cognizant of how their corporate actions directly impact people and places. If staff do not connect personally to the sustainability mission, they are less likely to support it.

Erika is an excellent example of someone who thoughtfully engaged all levels of an organization for support. She explained that in the green team she coleads, one professional each from twenty-five departments helps move sustainability initiatives forward within their own domain. This cross-functional approach alone is a powerful way to spread enlightenment throughout an organization.

She shared her mentality in approaching the team's work. "We are a mission-based organization focused on the environment and conservation, but if we're not inspiring our staff to participate in sustainability, not only at the job but also at home, we're not really doing service to our mission. The goal of the task force is to create unity in the identity that everybody who works there is a conservationist. If we're successful at ingraining that in our staff, then it's going to make the job easier because there's alignment."

Notice how earlier I gave an example of someone on a green team wanting to change people's sustainable behaviors at home, and I did not think that was the best way to focus their time and efforts given the nascent stage of environmental initiatives there? Here, though, we're talking about an organization much more advanced in such causes, and the nature of the mission and type of organization make this vision of impacting staff in their personal lives a more feasible and relevant goal.

As a group, Erika's green team works on larger sustainability topics requiring significant investment and executive endorsement. One was an overarching project with a large conservation component, and quite frankly a gruesome one! "We looked at data of birds striking windows in our city because it's a big problem. It's one of the leading causes of bird deaths. It seemed like a nice intersection between conservation and the sustainability of our building."

This is a smart move for raising awareness. The more you associate efforts with the organization's overall mission, the more palatable the changes you introduce. Staff are familiar with that flavor because, in theory, it's already sprinkled over everything people do daily. It's what executives report to their boards; it's what marketers spread on social media; it's what the product or service reflects. It should be a comfortable, if not exciting, place to start.

Erika continued, "For a large project to be successful, you need support from twenty-five departments, from the person greeting guests at the door to our CEO. One of the biggest barriers to sustainability in general is getting buy-in at the right levels at the right time. We are fortunate to be in an organization where our C-suite takes sustainability very seriously and I have access to our senior leadership team."

I asked her how she went from general support to specific backing for this project. Erika responded, "I was very democratic. The task force agreed, and then we reached out to other conservation organizations who were subject matter experts. They came out and helped us assess our site and risks, so we had the credibility of others in the field behind us."

Erika understood the need to allay any fears. "We anticipated there might be pushback because solving the bird strike problem entails making changes to the exteriors of windows. There's a set of windows along our executive floor, and they have beautiful views of the park. Somebody told me, you've got to be careful about James. He's going to be worried about his windows. I see these folks frequently, so I sidebar with him ahead of time to explain the film takes less than eight percent of the window's space and why it's important we install it."

Don't underestimate the power of behind-the-scenes politics. "By the time we got together for the yay or nay vote, I had spoken with everyone ahead of time. Everybody was an advocate, but they didn't know others were also. In fact, some of the folks who had been identified as possibly resisting turned out to already do something similar at home. A project like this costs hundreds of thousands of dollars, so we were fortunate to win approval."

Large expenditures and installations tend to be obvious to everyone because of how momentous and visible they are. This type of project is a crescendo of months, or even years, of planning, research, budgeting, and awareness building. Other initiatives, though, are in the minutia of everyday operations or pertinent to limited procedures. These too need a spotlight and buy-in.

COMMUNICATION GAPS

Much of the work I do with clients is on initiatives requiring behavior change. To a hammer everything's a nail, and if you haven't figured it out yet, my hammer is engaging employees and transforming culture.

This work requires appraising current perspectives and illuminating and educating toward a new solution or improved approach. I often find quite a disconnect in the basic comprehension of sustainability initiatives, which likely stems from a lack of information. As I mentioned in the previous section, organizational silos and inertia create barriers, preventing the flow of communication and understanding (as in compassion, respect, etc.). The top-down focus creates a *"need to know basis"* for sustainability programs. A campaign of illumination and clarification ensures staff know why and how.

Empathy precedes enlightenment. If the point is raising awareness, we must recognize we mostly start in a *"you don't know what you don't know"* place. What is the baseline awareness if we are to raise it?

ASSESSING THE DISCONNECT

A particularly revealing activity in my work is surveying staff across departments on existing and potential sustainability initiatives. I provide a list of common solutions to the problem at hand, whether those are in place or not. For each, I ask them to choose from the following list:

- I've never heard of this solution (or technique or technology, etc.).

- I am familiar with this solution, but our organization is not interested.

- I am familiar with this solution and our organization is considering it.

- We tried this but did not have good results.

- We tried this with mixed results.

- We've done (or installed, etc.) this, and it was effective and successful.

In theory, employees' responses reflect at least a degree of consistency. For example, to reduce energy, if the building has motion sensor lights in storage areas, janitorial closets, and less frequented hallways, you might expect the responses to range from "We tried this but did not have good results" to "We've done this, and it was effective and successful."

Interestingly, for one solution I get a range of all options across employee responses, meaning some think something has been done with success, while others think it's been done and failed or have never even heard of it. For solutions such as technical elements of building design, well sure, many staff will never have been exposed to pipes or electrical systems. However, I'm typically surveying about practices or equipment most, if not all, staff within the organization encounter regularly.

This survey is especially useful to show executives the lack of communication, awareness, participation (where a choice is offered), and acceptance across the organization. I work with global corporations' teams at the operational level and am witness to a stark disconnect between the website's sustainability page and what is evidenced on the ground.

This isn't meant to criticize those who tirelessly work to integrate sustainability into these organizations. It's meant to show others in the organization how much more attention and support those small sustainability teams need! The resources required to inform and educate can be easily overlooked in sustainability planning and budgeting.

Raising awareness isn't just evangelizing an idea. The right personality championing it may be enough. However, as sustainability becomes more sophisticated in an organization, or to ensure it does, the crusade to enlighten should be strategic, organized, and comprehensive.

Furthermore, like any of the principles covered in this book, it's not *"one and done."* Enlightening the organization evolves into training programs, ongoing communication, reminders about the importance of the initiative, and the role of each member of the organization in its success.

In the following chapters, best practices for raising awareness are broken down into classic question words:

- **Who** is the voice and who needs to receive the message?

- **What** is the message purpose, content, and design?

- **Where and when** should you get the word out?

- **How** can you make the message land and stick?

EXPONENTIAL IMPACT APPLICATION AND DISCUSSION

- What existing social and environmental initiatives suffer from a lack of communication and information? Remember, don't equate popularity and participation with success. In other words, if you hold a park cleanup activity, even the best enlightenment campaign is only going to get so many people to show up. Evaluate whether the campaign reached the right people, included the right details, and motivated participants. In the following chapters, we'll dive more into these components, but it's good to start with a list of initiatives or causes you want to illuminate for staff.

- Survey staff across departments about initiatives in place using a scale like that presented in this chapter. You might also use this as an empathy tool by adding questions to further explore the perspectives and opinions about these programs. Empathy is a key building block to enlightenment.

CHAPTER 11

WHO: IT TAKES
ALL KINDS

A GOOD PREACHER NEEDS A CONGREGATION

An executive at a client organization told me, "Aurora, no one makes staff care about this stuff like you do."

I make my living training teams on sustainability programs, but, as the commercial goes, that's priceless.

The connotation of this is not just that I'm a good evangelist for social and environmental initiatives, it's the word *"staff"* I most value in her statement. Sustainability is too often relegated to the executive team when all should have an opportunity to hear and participate in some way. Both the speaker and audience selection should be strategic and inclusive.

For the person sharing the message, passion is clearly a criterion for compelling delivery, but this does not always manifest as a skilled orator. For me, it does. For others, passion shines through one-on-one conversations and relationships. Nonetheless, a formal presentation should be part of the communication plan for new sustainability initiatives.

Don't leave this to the blah trainer staff are used to, or the canned video drill you use to check an ethics compliance box. I frequently hear positive feedback starting out with some version of "I thought this was going to be boring, but..." Why is it we have allowed professional education to be so very unappealing that low expectations are the *norm*?

I've been conducting sustainability training at convention centers and hotels since 2018. I stir up staff by connecting environmental problems with issues such as improving human health, increasing jobs for the community, and reducing negative impacts of pollution and chemicals on water and wildlife habitats. In this case, I'm a critical part of the equation, but I know it's ultimately not about me; it's about *who* is in the audience.

It's infuriating how hard it is to get management to agree to put the right employees in the room. I know beyond a shadow of a doubt cross-functional participation means lessons will have lasting impact and higher rates of success. When they don't allow for that, they have done themselves and the program a disservice. They only perpetuate siloed culture.

I acknowledge it's not realistic to train all staff in multihour, live workshops, but those invited become a first wave of collective enthusiasm and knowledge that washes over others and spreads awareness. Getting key decision makers to acquiesce takes finessing.

Here's how I do this:

- I explain possible operational changes so they connect the dots on who to invite, especially when I suggest people be in the room beyond the usual suspects (for example, asking marketing to attend training on something that seems purely operational).

- I encourage them to invite de facto leaders who have influence over their peers. These are approachable people everyone goes to when they're not sure how to do something at work.

- I recommend they invite key staff who might object so they feel included in the process and would be more willing to support, not prevent, change.

- I point out some employees are just dying to be invited to training like this, so don't assume staff will be bothered by this request.

- I remind them what I teach will need to be installed as new procedures. This one usually doesn't sink in until after I've taken them through three hours of content and they realize it will be difficult to effectively summarize, much less repeat, it.

A differentiating factor of organizations who realize benefits of the triple bottom line are those with a continuous improvement mindset, which translates into butts in seats in scheduled workshops. It's easy for organizations already doing a little bit to essentially say "nah, we're good" when asked to do a bit more. I recently spoke to a client a little over a year after training, and she told me the best practices are still in place and they've made new innovations since. She said, "It's all how you came in, got them excited, *and got everyone in the room and working together.*"

I cannot overstate the importance of getting all departments in the room. Even the best chef cannot make a great meal without the right ingredients. Staff is the ingredients.

OVERCOMING ENGAGEMENT CHALLENGES

THE POWER OF COMPLAINERS AND CONTENTION

When awareness first happens, the natural next step is *"who is to blame?"* (for example, "if that team would use the recap form the way they're supposed to, we wouldn't waste so much"). Earlier, I shared benefits of a survey exercise that exposes gaps in awareness and communication about existing initiatives. In addition to surveys, departmental focus groups are elucidating.

Start with a general conversation about the social or environmental issue at hand and related operational processes. Every department relies on input from and has output to other departments, so it's important to get to the point in the conversation where you ascertain the flow of information or materials among departments. This interchange, or lack thereof, is often a point of confusion and contention.

During focus groups, I pick up on dynamics within the department. While those in the room are usually just a selection of the total department, it's enlightening to see who's the complainer, who's the peacemaker, and who's the problem solver. This is crucial when deciding who is best positioned to do which task when it's time to implement change.

Opening lines of communication enables collaborative solutions to shared problems; therefore, the next step is cross-departmental activities. We work on a specific challenge or idea so the interaction is practical. Don't shortcut the process by squelching any complaining. Give it a bit of space but don't let it get unprofessional. Once people have vented a bit, steer them toward solutions.

In addition to the organizational obstacles, underlying personal barriers, which are less perceptible but nonetheless powerful, exist. For example, someone who does not believe climate change is real is asked to sit in on conversations about lowering carbon footprint. They could be doing the bare minimum to keep their job, but their disdain for the topic may be difficult to hide.

This creates a different kind of controversy, one potentially more volatile. It's natural to want to avoid an uncomfortable disruption, but if you discern problems brewing, ignoring it only makes it worse. As initiatives are more integrated, resisters grow more resentful. One view is their exit from the organization would help, not hurt culture, but it's unrealistic to fill an organization with only exactly like-minded people.

Recognize dissenting opinions are sources of valuable insights and solutions. Even if you rid your organization of them, you're still going to face them in the community, among shareholders, and within the customer base. Their opposing views can be leveraged to build empathy and design messages that will both reach and convert audiences.

WIN SOME FRIENDS

I facilitate cross-functional team activities or competitions to create camaraderie and cohesion. I bridge departmental gaps, which often led to the unsustainable custom in the first place. Employees see both their personal contribution to the cause and how the initiative is a mutual endeavor. This is how culture is transformed.

Diana launched a green team in a major New York City hotel in the 2000s, when sustainability was not nearly the in-demand topic it is today. She credits her position in the sales department with her ability to make this happen. "It's essential to have people skills in sustainability because it's all about relationships. I gathered one person from every department and started to see a shift in the way we were doing things and a change in the culture. It's about fostering those relationships, making departments that don't know each other work with others, working with the city, working with unions, and working with customers who are asking a thousand questions."

I've known many sustainability champions who were not exactly stand-in-front-of-a-room-of-people types be just as effective because they are good at something that is not as much my forte: building relationships at a grassroots level. Like Diana, they're willing to walk around and socialize an idea by getting to know people and listening. Their passion shows even if not accompanied by the volume at which mine does.

One of my favorite clients is a master at this. She is so naturally interested in people. When I'm with her at an account site, we can't get anywhere in the building in less than half an hour because of the number of people she runs into and asks about their family, their pets, their homes, their work—tidbits she remembers from brief encounters with them in past visits. Her heart for these people makes her a powerful advocate when overseeing corporate initiatives impacting them on any level.

Consider the role of relationships demonstrated in a study on engaging employees in impact programs.[1] The researchers explored why employees don't join in and 17 percent indicated "I didn't know anyone else who was participating."[2] This resonates on a personal level. I'm far more likely to go to a networking event if I can tag along with someone, which removes the awkwardness of standing around alone in a crowded room. There's joy in belonging.

In addition to passion and relationships, Diana shared other critical factors that magnified and strengthened the message. "We found buy-in isn't hard if the person selling it has credibility, authenticity, and believability." While these are foundational to messaging sustainability, they are not always enough to overcome some innate disadvantages.

DON'T SHOOT THE MESSENGER

Sometimes the person in charge of moving the needle on sustainability outcomes is passionate and authentic; however, they're still building credibility. They simply do not have the talent or characteristics traditionally accepted in a corporate environment, such as gender, age, education, and experience.

Selena was a young entry-level employee fortunate to land sustainability assignments early in her job at a financial institution. Banking is traditionally a male dominated industry.[3] Though this company was progressive in their environmental policies, the diversity and inclusion efforts fell short, which directly factored into Selena's ability to be effective in her role. "It can be harder to enlighten when you're going into it with disadvantages like being young or different in some way. My job at this company is to constantly try to bring up ideas, even when it gets shut down or doesn't land. It's harder because, a lot of the time, I'm one of the only females at the table and usually the youngest."

Those with such disadvantages need to cultivate patience and persistence, but it also helps if someone is willing to mentor and support them along the way.

Presentation without representation happens when you educate an organization on a topic, particularly a social impact topic, and the people conveying the message have no lived experience, much less empathy, for the problem. In fact, they may even deny there's a problem at all.

Things get lost in translation. Sometimes the person put in the position of conveying the "*why*" does not have enough fervor to be convincing. They lack detailed knowledge; therefore, they cannot answer nuanced questions. Partner with someone in the department and test out the vernacular and technical elements to make sure they bring about clarity, not perplexity.

Speaking of vernacular, us sustainability nerds easily overwhelm our audience. We geek out on technicalities and think the big words and acronyms we learned must be used. It's often not at all necessary to engage staff on a topic and change their minds. In fact, the more you use unapproachable language, the less, well, approachable you are.

"The more you use unapproachable language, the less, well, approachable you are."

I continually speak with sustainability specialists who talk over and around others. That is not their intention; they are simply unaware how unapproachable, esoteric, and even downright irrelevant their message is. I'm sure I also fall into this trap when I'm not watching my step.

Similarly, some *"experts"* may need to unlearn what they were so sure was the right answer. On the operational side, this is confronting the *"we've always done it this way"* mentality. Sustainability requires an open mind, a willingness to accept the answer to a problem may be one you never considered, even if you have been in your field for a long time.

I face this when I train executive chefs. They are accustomed to being the king of their domain, and the expressions on their faces screams, *"Who are you to come in here and tell me how to do my job?"*

I merely point out, without direct criticism, how the world around them evolved and they stayed the same. Fortunately, most people are reasonable enough to see the light and change their ways when presented options in a professional and reasonable manner.

From raising awareness to providing education on process change, those positioned to share the *"why"* should be authentic, credible, approachable, and sincere. Whether downright objectors, passive participants, or potential champions, anyone who will be impacted by sustainability initiatives should be targeted in the messaging strategy.

EXPONENTIAL IMPACT APPLICATION AND DISCUSSION

- Identify speakers and videos that will capture attention and raise awareness. Curate a list of go-to resources from the gobs of excellent and brief explainer videos online and compelling speakers on the topic of sustainability.

- Identify who should be in the room when it comes to the following:

  o Designing the program: these people have a real sense of the strategic value of an initiative. They also tend to be people who have a better understanding of the overall organizational dynamic—either due to their position, their longevity with the organization, or their relationships.

  o Implementing the program: these people are action and project management oriented. They will not be blinded by the passion of the idea. They may care deeply, but their natural talents take them straight to the place of "okay, how do we make this happen?"

o Cheerleading the program: these people may not be part of design or implementation because they are lower level or have a narrow job focus that does not entail the specific tasks required. However, they are passionate supporters who bring energy and infectious enthusiasm to the table.

o Sabotaging the program: these are the grumblers and dissenters who, even if unintentionally, will be the downfall of your best-laid plans. They must be invited and drawn out. They can very easily switch from your greatest enemy to your greatest advocate!

- Who are the internal message bearers? In addition to a library of external resources, who are the internal speakers and relationship builders who can be trusted to spread and reinforce the message?

- For each of those internal champions, what potential challenges might they face? Their age? Their position in the organization? Their background? Help them recognize these so they can be patient and intentional as they work to share information and change attitudes.

CHAPTER 12

WHAT: CAMPAIGN
FOR CHANGE

CHAMPION AS CURATOR

Have you ever scrolled through social media and something you'd been thinking you needed (but never said out loud) suddenly appeared in your feed? Despite the creepy coincidence, advertisements only have about two seconds to capture your attention, so whatever they put in front of you must be spectacular. Otherwise, the next attention grabber will pull you away from them.

Integrating sustainability in an organization requires disseminating a lot of information and instruction to people already overwhelmed with content and concerns. The targeted audience isn't necessarily demanding what you're selling, although some are secretly dreaming it will come along when the missive appears at an opportune moment.

The message needs defined objectives and outcomes, which can range from convincing others to comply with an unfamiliar policy, generating buzz on a new initiative, or bursting the bubble of myopic thinking. As such, content should be thoughtfully designed to meet those goals and cut through the noise of daily organizational life.

It takes coaxing to move an organization from the status quo to the utopia you might envision. Ideally, you must drive change in behavior and practice, but to get there, you need intermediate objectives like changing their minds and urgency level. In content design, to achieve the ultimate goal of social or environmental impact, you need to consider the philosophical or attitudinal barriers.

Sustainability content creation boils down to:

- Raising awareness.

    This is knowledge for knowledge's sake such as:

    o   opening eyes to new concepts,

    o   building vocabulary,

    o   sparking curiosity, and

    o   garnering general interest.

    If the issues are on the complex end of the sustainability spectrum, it's best to first develop familiarity with approachable concepts such as supporting a local charity or cleaning a nearby park.

- Overcoming apathy.

  Staff may be aware of the problem but still have an *"it's not my job"* or *"I don't care"* mentality about initiatives. They deflect responsibility for what's happening in the world. It's not likely you'll convert them to passionate supporters, but at least expose their own part in the problem *and* the solution.

- Educating and instructing.

  Some employees need to be equipped to do the job. This content is more about operations and steps to follow, more technical and in-depth. Nonetheless, it must be accessible and take the previous two points into consideration.

- Driving compliance.

  Increasingly, sustainability initiatives are tied to mandatory policies or even law. Regulations and contracts are forceful mechanisms to get people to account for their impact. This is where *"because I said so"* is a legitimate approach, but that doesn't mean you can't soften the blow with increased awareness and decreased apathy.

- Bursting the bubble.

  In this case, their *"head is in the sand"* and they have been unwilling to accept a reality outside their own experience. It's hard for those who personally benefit from societal systems to accept that the apparatus is flawed. Select content with a touch of shock factor without freaking people out too much.

- Making the business case.

  Prove operational efficiencies, brand value, risk avoidance, and other business gains. Environmental, social, and governance (ESG) has become an expected component of financial accounting for publicly traded companies. For example, any firm in the supply chain of corporations based in Europe must now meet stringent requirements enacted in recent years.

- Prompting an individual call to action.

  You may wish to draw people in as active participants, to volunteer, raise their hand, and show up. Motivating people to go above and beyond leads to successful initiatives and culture development.

POSITIONING THE MESSAGE

Sustainability messaging can contain a plethora of issues, research, and solutions. Limit the initial enlightenment campaign to what most supports existing priorities. Even once you narrow down the issues, you still have literally volumes of sources from which to draw content. What tugs at my heart may not tug at yours. The best way to convince people to care about sustainability is to make it relevant to their daily lives and work. This was essentially the point of the previous section on empathy, which carries over to Enlighten because it dictates the message you craft.

Donna, who I introduced earlier, tried to get new recycling initiatives off the ground at the distribution center. She discovered the importance of curating the right content for coworkers.

"At first, I was eager and pushing a pallet take-back program. None of it was getting through. Why don't they care? Then I focused on the relationship of my idea to an internal assessment of our distribution operations. Turns out there was also a connection to customer feedback we were struggling to address. This highlighted the importance of sustainability and engaged departments in a new way. When the sales team realized the opportunity to gain customer loyalty, they perked up. When the warehouse team learned how much energy and water is saved, they were less reluctant to adopt the program."

Pulling this off requires research. Ideally, we instill a culture of curiosity and continual learning among those most likely to champion sustainability initiatives. I recommend all members of a green team be assigned a research task. When I seek information on a topic, I start with Google (or your preferred search engine). Most people would not hesitate to Google *"how do I change the filter in my car?"* or *"gluten-free brownie recipe"* but will shut down when faced with dilemmas like *"which supply chains have slave labor?"* or *"what business activities create the most carbon emissions?"*

A search may result in sponsored or questionable results, but at least you've started the journey. Watch a brief explainer video or read a short article for quick learning. Eventually, make your way to content produced by nonprofits, academic institutions, or reputable media companies. For example, rely on publications from World Wildlife Fund, Nature Conservancy, and other global organizations devoted to social and environmental causes. Blogs and reports produced by corporations can also be helpful. Corporations can afford to fund quality research, which can be expensive. Keep in mind, however, the intent may ultimately be to sell you a service or product. I've referenced a number of these in this book.

Once you have a library of content, you still need to cull it down. Remember what we learned from Valerie earlier: "my thing isn't their thing." Filter content through empathy to extract the best nuggets for the audience. If the communication bar is set too high, no one will come to the trough, much less drink.

Content can address your most staunch objectors or recruit those most likely to convert into cheerleaders. Start with their objections and motivators and let that qualify the best data and stories. For example, if presenting to executives focused on market growth, illustrate data tying sustainability to desirable market segments. Show them 70 percent of millennials and Gen Z believe brands should "do more to help them live a sustainable lifestyle."[1] A compelling argument can be made to support investments in new environmental product features, enhanced labeling, or pursuing an eco-certification.

CONTENT IS A FOUR COURSE MEAL

People don't like change and don't like feeling they are, or were, wrong about something. Sustainability almost always means causing this discomfort. You have to pry their mindset from entrenched thinking. Pointing out common fallacies about an issue can reset the baseline for acceptable performance and open people up to change.

For example, as the cause of food waste has gained popularity in recent years, many foodservice organizations and average consumers have started composting. While the case for composting is strong, we must look forward to the next round of enlightenment.

Namely, in the food waste–reduction methodology, composting is a vital part of the equation, but better steps come first. I have worked with teams who thought because they were composting, they could legitimately say *"we don't have food waste."* I responded by showing the bigger picture of what food waste is and techniques they have yet to employ (for example, prevention through portion control and donating excess food to those facing food insecurity).

This is unpleasant initially because acknowledging they have more to do means first accepting their accomplishments haven't been enough. At least that's how the message touches them. I recognize this stings people, so my approach is to couch new realities in terms and concepts designed to expand their thinking.

Sustainability can be like fitting a size ten foot into a size six shoe. You're not going to shrink the foot (your sustainability ambitions or requirements), and if you try to jam that foot into that shoe, it's going to hurt. You must stretch the leather of the shoe, or stretch the mindsets of people to contain more perspectives than they had going in.

When you broach the topic with a *"why"* that resonates, you open the door for people to question their assumptions. For example, food donation in hospitality is almost universally associated with strong misconceptions. Foodservice operators have long resisted donating food for fear of liability. *"We could get sued"* or *"It's against the law"* is the mantra echoing in the kitchens of hotels, restaurants, convention centers, and other hospitality businesses.

First, you open the door to the topic by sharing hunger rates in the city, state, or region. It is not unusual to have people in the audience (for example, line cooks, stewards, janitors, and servers) who grew up or currently live in areas hardest hit by food insecurity. This engages the heart.

Next, confront the myth or other type of *"we've always done it this way"* thinking. When conducting training, I ask staff, "Do you think the company can be sued for donating food?" Typically, about ninety percent of the hands in the room go up.

In the case of food donation, a federal law (in the US and in other countries) protects hospitality companies from liability when they donate in good faith, using the normal food safety rules they use to serve guests, to nonprofits who serve food to the community. Not only that, but in some places (for example, California) it is now the law that hospitality companies donate safe, excess food.

This surprises people. Even more shocking is the federal law has been in place since 1996 and, as of recently, has never once been tried in court. This means not only is there a law to protect the hospitality industry, but the fear of getting sued has no legal precedent. It's eye-opening for people to realize their beliefs were based on a myth! Especially a belief pervading an entire industry which has prevented it from positively impacting communities facing hunger.

Now, we can move forward with solutions. Once you lay the foundation of a solid why, especially one so many will be personally drawn to (reducing food insecurity in your local community), and you remove doubts and fears with something rather indisputable (a federal or state law), staff will more quickly get down to the nuts and bolts of figuring out how to safely donate.

Enlightenment sets up teams and departments to embrace change. Change is scary and most people will avoid it so a compelling awareness-raising campaign will go a long way in convincing people to even consider seeing the world differently, much less altering behavior and habits.

"Enlightenment sets up teams and departments to embrace change."

CONTENT CAUTIONS

Authenticity is critical in sustainability content. If you do not practice what you preach, your words will ring hollow and not garner attention.

I taught a course on launching and managing green teams in which students researched their employer's sustainability claims. I've lost count of the number of times I heard statements such as, *"I didn't know we did that"* or *"They don't do that at our branch."* This leads to an incongruent experience that, at best, erodes culture and, at worst, creates a reputational risk.

When that contrasting experience happens outside the organization, it is perceived as greenwashing. Greenwashing is the exaggeration or falsification of social and environmental benefits, results, or features. The United Nations calls it "misleading" and warns it can show up in a variety of ways, including claiming progress without a plan to back it up, vague claims and explanations, using unregulated terms like *"green,"* shining a light on a positive area while hiding or ignoring negative impacts, and making claims that are not even relevant to the product or operation.[2] The average consumer is getting savvy, and the more people know, the more they will spot, and call you out on, bullsh*t.

With an increase in the mentions of greenwashing in the media, companies are, rightfully so, concerned about getting called out, particularly when it leads to action taken by federal agencies, the Better Business Bureau, or watchdog groups.

Some startling statistics on the prevalence of this are presented in the 2023 report on greenwashing by RepRisk. Specifically, oil and gas tend to dominate the examples, but travel, airlines, and banking have seen increases as a percentage of overall claims investigated. A 70 percent increase in greenwashing in the banking and financial services sector alone demonstrates this is not just a problem for entities that mine or manufacture stuff.[3]

Among common social issues, poor employment conditions, human rights abuses, and corporate complicity topped the charts of questionable claims, along with occupational health and safety issues and impacts on community (such as pollution and water quality).[4]

If you have been angered by catching a company greenwashing, my counsel is to consider the full story. The tendency is to see it as nefarious. We imagine corporate leaders sitting in a boardroom maniacally laughing and plotting the end of the world. No, that is not how greenwashing happens. Okay, maybe instances of unscrupulous executives outright lying and perpetrating fraud have led to it. Mostly though, greenwashing is probably a result of:

- **Siloed and Globally Complex Operations**

   A great example of this is when, a few years back, H&M was promoting an in-store clothing recycling program. Customers could bring old clothes into the store, and H&M would donate or repurpose them. What a brilliant tactic to get people into the store and a clever way to deal with the negative notions of throwaway fashion that has filled our wardrobes with practically single-use items.

   Unfortunately, it hit the news that an H&M warehouse was caught burning excess inventory. Headlines made it sound as though H&M had intentionally duped the world; however, burning inventory has been a common practice in the industry for decades.[5] That doesn't make it right, but in all probability employees who burned those items work for a third-party warehouse and were never included in specific training on sustainability. Most likely, a policy written in difficult to understand language was taped on a wall somewhere. The person who lit the match may not even be literate.

- **Misinterpretation**

Marketing and sales oversee most messaging and customer-facing elements of sustainability. They are not versed in technical details and are left to interpret, or spin, features or results through their lens, which is to drive clicks, visits, and sales. One example of this drives me nuts. It is an ad for a dishwasher soap pod claiming it's good to run your dishwasher every day, even if it's not full.[6] The audacity of this company to argue this is good for the planet!

When journalists report on companies caught in the act of greenwashing, they rarely unpack the error at a granular level. Without access to internal culprits, how could they? Transparency is a hallmark of avoiding greenwashing risk.

With my clients, I watch for potentially misleading comments in collateral and explain how to appropriately use terms. I can speculate where things fell apart. For instance, someone in marketing may have copy written and took a bit of license (probably without realizing it). That doesn't excuse the action; it reveals a leak to plug.

- **Fine Print**

Companies take advantage of loopholes and the lack of clear policy that would prevent their actions. For example, thanks to USDA rules, for years Americans have been eating meat labeled "Product of the USA" that was born, raised, and even slaughtered in other countries. As long as meat from other countries went to a USDA-inspected plant where it would be mixed with other meat (from the US and other countries), it could be labeled as "Product of the USA."[7]

If you're passionate about ethical farming, the distinction matters because in one possible scenario the cattle are shipped from other countries. That's terribly distressing to the animal and defeats the purpose of supposed humane or regenerative practices.

New information comes to light all the time that might recast knowledge we so vehemently believed. That's to be expected, but don't get sloppy in the research or representation of sustainability issues or your organization's impact. It's bad enough to do this to consumers, but employees are also watching. When sharing information during awareness raising and training, depend on reliable, up-to-date resources, and deliver it from an authentic stance.

EXPONENTIAL IMPACT APPLICATION AND DISCUSSION

- What is the organizational context you should be cognizant of in designing your message?

- What are the objections and attitudes your content will need to confront head on? What might be addressed in a more surreptitious way?

- What are examples of greenwashing you have noticed from other brands? If your organization is already communicating, internally or externally, about social or environmental issues, what are the potential risks of perceived or real greenwashing?

- What is the ultimate call to action or desired outcome of the message or training? Using the food waste example outlined below, write out a content plan for an initiative you are trying to champion.

At the beginning of this chapter, I provided a list of what content boils down to. Below I have given examples to inspire you to map out your own messaging strategy. In this scenario, a foodservice organization was rolling out a comprehensive program on food waste reduction that included composting, food donation, and improved inventory management.

- Raise awareness. Share basic food waste concepts and statistics.
  - o For example,
    - In the US we waste 38 percent of our food.[8]
    - In the US, food waste takes up 24 percent of landfills, and 22 percent of all fresh water is used to grow crops that never get eaten.[9]

  - o Even better, use visual information put together by other organizations to display basic facts. For example, the Food and Agriculture Organization of United Nations published a cute video demonstrating how food waste occurs along the entire supply chain.[10]

- Educate and instruct. Kitchen staff need to be cognizant of compost processes such as what to compost (this can vary—for example, some composters will accept certain to-go containers while others will not). Equally important is what not to compost (for example, gloves and hairnets will cause a high rate of contamination).

- Drive compliance. Staff must be aware of relevant laws dictating whether donation is optional or mandatory, as well as laws on food safety and handling. Additionally, inform staff of internal policies, such as what type of containers are allowed for donation, who signs off on processes, and what food items local organizations accept.

- Overcome apathy. Go from informative to eye-opening! For example, I show an attention-grabbing chart with the amount of water used in the production of certain foods.[11] This jolts the room, especially when presented in drought prone areas. If staff are already sold on the importance of one topic (for example, water conservation), use that to highlight other problems.

- Burst the bubble. For those who have not taken time to connect the dots of food waste with community health, the following reveal the stark reality some are facing:

o   Hunger rates in the nearby community. If it's available, I find data broken down by neighborhood, or by segments such as the elderly or children. In the US, for some towns or for some demographics, food insecurity can be as much as double the national average.

o   Data from food waste audits (whether internal or from similar organizations) showing just how much food is wasted. When you juxtapose this with the above, it is difficult to deny the problem, and it's kind of nuts the organization is not doing more to alleviate it by donating excess food.

- Make the business case. Even the most basic data tells a compelling story. In professional kitchens, I frequently see handwritten spoilage logs hanging near storerooms or walk-in refrigerators. I convert a page of it into a digital format and do basic sorting and subtotaling to quickly show foods most wasted. While staff probably have an intuitive sense of what those are, hard data enables them to justify an investment in solutions (for example, inventory tracking technology or containers that better preserve food).

- Individual call to action. Once people get excited about the topic, they begin to identify new and creative ways to prevent or efficiently manage food waste. I hear staff say, "I think we donate food, but I'm not sure how or where it goes." If they are not responsible for handling the food, they are excluded from the messaging; however, once they are informed, they want to help out, whether by filling in during hectic shifts or signing up to help out at the food bank over the weekend.

It would be easy to think a one-size-fits-all for employee-facing sustainability messaging and content would work. However, as you can see, the content of the message can be strategically and operationally aligned to achieve a specific purpose. Going along with this is the timing and placement of messages, which we turn to next.

CHAPTER 13

WHERE AND WHEN: GETTING THE WORD OUT

PUSH VS. PULL

In the previous chapter, I opened with the analogy of seeing ads that prompt a new urge. A sponsored ad in your social media feed, a television commercial between plays of your favorite sport, or a billboard you stare at during rush hour illustrate good advertising. In the classic push strategy, marketers drive demand by being where and when the potential customer is.

On the other hand, if you've been specifically thinking about purchasing an item, you go to websites to learn more about products, read reviews, and see alternative features. In this case, the marketer has ensured you can pull the details you need to complete a transaction. Pull makes the sought-after information available where and when the market proactively seeks it and leads to a positive customer experience and increased loyalty.

The sustainability equivalent of this is demonstrated in my experience with the client who rolled out an e-waste policy. After we guided a committee through drafting a clear guideline, we created a ten-minute video to accompany the announcement. The training video highlighted social and environmental problems occurring when electronics, components, and accessories are not properly refurbished or recycled. The video also explained the company's process, which was important since there were alternative paths depending on the type of item (for example, laptop, keyboard, chargers) and where the employee works (for example, remote, headquarters, satellite office).

The email went out companywide to coincide with National Recycling Day. Perfect timing. The policy was attached and the video hyperlinked to an internal storage location. Months later in a focus group of about fifteen participants, I asked for a show of hands for how many read the policy. About three quarters of the hands went up. I asked how many viewed the video. Two hands went up.

What came next proved exactly what I had predicted. They started asking where to find the video. It became clear they hadn't even noticed there was a video to watch. It was a few paragraphs down in the email and did not stand out. Unfortunately, even the sustainability team had to dig a bit to find the location where the video could be accessed. Fortunately, this prompted a productive conversation about where content like this should be stored in the future.

The company pushed information out to staff once; however, they needed to continue to push out reminders from time to time, as well as make it easy for employees to find and pull. If the pushed message is appealing and becomes integrated into corporate rituals, people will eventually seek it out.

CAPTIVE AUDIENCE

Awareness building sometimes assumes we have a built-in audience. Yes, if they are sitting in a training session, then people listen, or at least pretend to. My work often entails presenting to a group of managers and staff who have been told to be in the room. The easy part is getting the desired response once they're in the room. The hard part is establishing *when* they'll get in the room.

Until sustainability is integrated into operations and accountability, it will be seen as optional, so getting leadership to set aside time for staff to be in training is one of the most difficult hurdles I have to overcome. Managers acknowledge training is important but sometimes insist on waiting for some milestone or another. For example, they want to delay until they have budget to buy new equipment, or until a director position is filled, or until the *"busy season"* is over. The reality is, if you let that continue, training will never happen. The *"busy season"* is an oxymoron because the chaos of business never ends. Even when things are relatively slower, other projects or tasks take precedence.

In the effort to engage and retain employees, we must acknowledge the time commitment needed. In the eyes of management, it may be unreasonable to hold a four-hour training session on a topic, even when it is generally acknowledged to be an important one.

Employees don't see it that way. In the 2023 *Voice of the American Workforce Survey Report,* when logistics and manufacturing employees were surveyed, an average of about 30 percent indicated they would invest one to two hours per week in learning new skills, and as much as about 27 percent would invest five to ten hours.[1]

Leverage a moment when everyone pays attention to other messages such as all staff meetings or newsletters. This creates a habit of integrating sustainability into ongoing communications. In these cases, you'll want the message to be brief. It's so tempting for sustainability champions to insist they must get in all the messaging at once. In the right scenario, you can get people to pay attention for hours. In some cases, I run three-to-six-hour workshops, but most times, spoon-feeding the content is more apropos. I admit this is a challenge, but due to my brand promise, I've trained myself and my team to be okay with bite-sized pieces of information doled out over time.

PUT IT ON A DIMMER SWITCH

Timing is everything with initiative rollouts. I found bringing sustainability awareness to organizations is like walking into a room and flipping on the lights. People get used to the dark and believe all they can see is all there is to see. When that light comes on, it can be blinding. It's difficult for people to take in the reality of all they have done or are doing to cause harm. The reaction is denial and finger-pointing.

> *"People get used to the dark and believe all they can see is all there is to see. When that light comes on, it can be blinding."*

Put awareness and education on a dimmer switch. As you slowly bring up the lights, acclimate people to truth and solutions. Stage the awareness campaign so it's not a floodlight. Too much is too much. Heaviness brings people down, and sustainability needs a lot of positivism and hope to survive!

In some cases, the team is already on the journey and so proud of what they've done. It's a *"we're all better now"* belief. They show me their progress with anticipation of my *"attagirl"* response. I know they have a long way to go, but that's not the time or place for correction. Any moment someone shares their new revelation or practice is a reason to celebrate. The real victory is their new mentality.

Many sustainability initiatives are rolled out in a voluntary, *"wouldn't it be nice if we all..."* manner, so we use signage, social media, newsletters, and other communication pushed out to audiences whose mindset and behavior we wish to influence. You rely on someone on the other end to be interested enough to read or click to learn more. That's a big leap.

While it would be lovely for people to just inherently care and gravitate toward your initiative, you likely need to plan and stage messaging much the way an advertiser does to get the attention of consumers. The job of raising awareness involves planting seeds, watering them, and nourishing relationships.

USE SPOKESPEOPLE

In a best-case scenario, you've pulled together a group of people into some sort of green team, which often starts out as a group of passionate members, but also perhaps even neutral or disinterested people who were told to be there. Either way, you've got them in a room and it's time to enlighten.

Earlier you met Diana, who launched and led sustainability in hotels. She had to first engage her green team so they could then socialize ideas and enlighten all staff. She said, "The biggest impact is to just talk to people and educate them on how important it is for us to look at the world with a different eye, to see how we can tweak the things we do to make a big change. This is a small step with a big impact because those individuals started to communicate with their own departments the importance of looking at things differently. Then they started coming up with suggestions to change hotel operations. It changed the minds of people who had worked there for twenty-five years."

Conversations can happen over lunch, in the hallway, or in other meetings. These are informal spaces where the message is spread. They are organic, unscripted, and even spontaneous, which means they are laden with honesty and credibility. On the other hand, this is how rumors spread, myths pervade, and misunderstandings and criticisms get out of hand. It's important to stay as tapped into these conversations as possible, as an opportunity to listen, but also to steer the talk to truth and positivity.

If you are the champion, be patient and assertive where and when you are able. Consistency pays off. Where? In every executive or team meeting. When? Every chance you get.

DON'T PLAY HARD TO GET

Researchers at WeSpire asked employees why they don't participate in impact programs (for example, volunteerism, wellness). The top response was "I didn't know about the opportunity to participate"; 11 percent claim they did not know how to sign up.[2] This underscores the vital role of a communication plan that addresses the why, but also the where, when, and how of sustainability programs.

This study also showed how people like to receive information about programs. Surprisingly, email came out on top (54 percent) as well as learning about it from friends or managers (38 and 36 percent respectively). Lower on the list were signs in the building, intranet, internal social platforms, and online apps.[3]

Of course, the industry and age group of your audience will dictate preferences or even limitations on what's available to you. For example, in the hospitality world, physical signage around buildings is a must. In a knowledge industry, naturally emails make more sense.

Myra oversees a sustainability team in an office building with many tenants and employees. They talked about efforts to insert sustainability every chance they get. "We have a newsletter every month highlighting sustainability and heroes in the building. We have visuals in the break rooms. We have monitors cycling through screens highlighting sustainability. When we host tenant events on our terrace, we use all sustainable materials and donate excess food. We present at staff meetings throughout the building. We have an innovation corner where we talk about anything related to sustainability."

Even with all that, projects and people fall through the cracks. Myra continued, "Communication is such a hard part. Making sure we have that constant stream of what we're doing is helpful. Even if you do a newsletter, speak at all staff meetings, and your task force members are out communicating, there'll always be that one person who is like, 'Well, I didn't know, I didn't hear.'"

Like the analogy of planting and nurturing seeds, this

doesn't happen overnight. Be patient and persistent in your messaging strategy and tactics.

EXPONENTIAL IMPACT APPLICATION AND DISCUSSION

- List out the moments and meetings where you can leverage a captive audience to share information on sustainability programs.

- When is the best time of day to reach targeted internal audiences with messages about initiatives and opportunities to participate? Consider shift starts, busy and hectic times, and when employees can pay the best attention to the message.

- Where are staff most likely to notice and absorb messages about sustainability initiatives?

- If someone interested in sustainability joined your organization as a new employee today, how easily would they find information on what your organization is doing overall? What about as it pertains to their location, department, or role?

CHAPTER 14

HOW: STICK THE LANDING

COMING IN HOT VS. A PEACEFUL APPROACH

Coldplay released a sustainability report.[1] For millions of fans, this may have been the first time they saw such a thing. If someone admires Coldplay but was on the fence about aspects of sustainability, this nudge activated an interest in environmental issues. The online report was easy to navigate, visually stunning, and chock-full of data-driven results. The packaging of their message was stunning. I wanted to open it and read more.

At that time, some sustainability professionals started trashing Coldplay's efforts and poking holes in every part of the reporting they could. Extremists ruin it for the rest of us. The *"Earth is burning and the sky is falling"* style urgency is a turn off. The average person will tune it out and not engage in a dialogue, much less change their behavior. Messages couched in blame and shame is not the way to endear people to our cause.

The person trying to champion sustainability in an organization may have passion and worry others don't care enough, so they come in full throttle with all the heaviness of the world's problems. It's just too much to take. They may believe fear tactics are necessary to lead change. In communication with staff and stakeholders, we must evaluate the packaging in which the message is delivered.

I developed an approach to better present complex and loaded topics. I call it my PEACE framework:

- **P**ractical: Aim to attract and educate those who likely have little or no formal training in sustainability. They are not interested in philosophical or theoretical content; they seek checklists to take steps toward sustainability.

- **E**conomical: Emphasize the strategic value of sustainability as well as the business cases of operational efficiency, customer acquisition, risk mitigation, and employee engagement.

- **A**pproachable: Be a voice of positivity, a friendly resource who brings hope and uses a tone appealing to a wider audience, including those at the lowest levels of organizations.

- **C**elebrate: Cast the employee as the hero of the story. Encourage people to feel pride and accomplishment in their team, themselves, their community, their organization. Make them feel good about the next step, not bad for the previous ones.

- **E**njoyable: Sustainability is an uphill battle. We can't change that, but as we climb the mountain, let's experience purpose, professional growth, camaraderie, fun, inspiration, and joy.

The essence of this is how people *experience* sustainability. The PEACE framework leads to exponential impact!

It's important the topic go from *"Why do we have to attend this four-hour training?"* to "Wow, I didn't know this was such a problem, much less that I can be a part of solving it." I approach it in the way I would want to receive it. Tell me why it matters I perform this task, change this process, or do something differently. Make it relevant and actionable.

Ways to ensure the message is packaged effectively are to:

- Make it recognizable!

- Make it visual!

- Make it tactile!

MAKE IT RECOGNIZABLE!

Sustainability nerds get hung up on specific terminology or ways of presenting social and environmental concepts.

When they remain inflexible in how they communicate those, they create noise, not possibility. They want their words to carry the weight of the problems we need to solve. Watered down words dilute a message. However, turning on the fire hose and inundating everyone with jargon and acronyms is not the antidote. Not only have we overwhelmed the audience with the weight of the world's ills, we make them uncomfortable by speaking a language they don't understand.

Instead, we need to scaffold messages using recognizable terms. Pull from the language already dictating their responsibility. Revisit the organization's mission, values, goals, and strategy to learn the language resonating with stakeholders. An executive, at any given moment, has many urgent issues, so if you want yours to cut through, use words and concepts sure to trigger a response.

For example, if growing sales is the imperative of the day, demonstrate how sustainability product innovations lead to opening new markets or better appealing to key customer demographics. If risk factors are top of mind, show how sustainability reduces risks (for example, a focus on health and safety). If a key executive is overseeing an office expansion, introduce how sustainability naturally fits into decisions and could enhance the overall outcome (for example, choosing more efficient lighting and equipment, designing layouts that improve both employee health and productivity, selecting furnishings produced by a small diverse supplier).

If you frame ideas in unknown or irrelevant terms, your audience may not click into a gear of curiosity. On the other hand, if you contextualize using empathy, like how the stock market responds or what competitors are doing, the door is open to also include new terms and concepts.

As a sustainability expert, or someone on that journey, it's easy to get caught up in needing to use all this knowledge you've obtained and to use it precisely. If your audience doesn't know any better, those semantics muddle the message. Despite nuances in terminology, when I'm training hospitality staff, the distinction between food insecurity and hunger or aerobic and anaerobic composting doesn't matter in terms of what will change in their daily routine nor how it grips their hearts to care.

It doesn't help that when things are new, the experts are still trying to figure out uniform vernacular. Until then, companies throw around buzzwords and add to the chaos. For example, when words like carbon neutral and net-zero were first rising in popularity, people struggled to understand the difference. With more than half a dozen different terms associated with various states of carbon or greenhouse gas (GHG) emissions reductions, removals, and offsets, we're asking a lot of people to know anywhere near as much as we might on the topic.[2]

I wrote a carbon emissions module for a course, and an expert on the input team insisted we explain a lot of technicalities. I pushed back and reminded him the learners were beginners. Coming into this they wouldn't even know what GHGs are. It's a ten-minute learning video, which is insufficient to lay enough of the groundwork we'd need to go deeper on the topic. We would be asking these learners to comprehend and act on information unrelated to what drove them to the course in the first place.

When choosing language, start with the landing objectives, identify the thought process or behavior change you desire, then find the simplest language possible to achieve that.

MAKE IT VISUAL!

Like the words chosen, icons and images drive home points and illicit responses. People love a good infographic, and these can be especially helpful in delivering social and environmental facts and figures. A graphical representation shows a complex, systems view and ripple effects of actions. I once again reference the SDGs as a brilliant example of how a visual conveys so much, so quickly, and so effectively. Many corporate entities and nonprofits now tie their sustainability initiatives to these seventeen categories and use the iconography provided by the United Nations.

Visuals illustrate the bigger picture of complex concepts. A holistic view helps people see the world less myopically. For example, Jack worked in a technology office park and tried to convince people to not be flippant about tossing cigarette butts on the ground. He figured out if he could show them the direct impact on local bodies of water, it might change behavior. The fact that the bay was not safe for swimming was a big deal, so he showed how small items of plastic end up in storm drains, wash into the ocean, break down, and detrimentally alter water quality and marine life. A simplistic visual diagram proved this. Combined with new cigarette butt collection spots and signage, it became a no-brainer to properly dispose of this trash.

Some aspects of sustainability aren't seen with one's eyes or the end user is so far removed from the source it's difficult to fathom the problem. For example, carbon emissions reduction may ultimately lead to breathing cleaner air and improved human health, but it's hard for people to connect with the significance if they are not personally seeing or experiencing polluted air.

In the New York hotel where Diana worked, she used video to compel staff to care about waste. "When I arrived, there was no recycling. We put the right receptacles in the right place, and we emphasized how important recycling was. We would go to each department and show a video of Staten Island's landfill and how you could see it from space. That hit home for people who have been New Yorkers for many years and have lived in or passed by Staten Island. Something they once thought was extra work and that they should get paid more for was now part of regular operations."

Visuals are indisputable! Most of the time when I'm brought into a hotel or venue, the executive chef is in denial. They're convinced what they're doing is enough.

They tend to have a limited view—figuratively and literally. In one sense, they see only their span of control and tend to discount the role other departments play in waste reduction. In another sense, they literally do not see the full picture. They often are in the kitchen or elsewhere when food is served and cleared.

I found photos are powerful in this regard. It's not uncommon for an executive chef to claim there is no waste when others clearly see the waste. Even if they don't, I do. My opinion doesn't count for much, but photos don't lie. If a picture speaks a thousand words, it can likely save a thousand dollars by revealing wasteful and inefficient habits. If a picture is worth a thousand words, a video is worth a million! It's important to capture the status quo and play it back so everyone can see it. Even if they see it or know what the process is supposed to be, this shows everyone the reality.

"If we're in it all together, then no one person is in trouble and it's easier for everyone to see past the mistakes and get down to solving the problem."

The key is not to use data or images punitively. If you destroy trust and halt communication, your sustainability initiatives will not be successful. I introduce the photos along with team activities in which solutions are immediately identified. For example, I often hear from chefs that charcuterie boards are popular and not a problem. I hear from dishwashers how much of it ends up in the trash.

The photos allow for a lighthearted tone, sort of a collective admitting of *"oh my, look what we've been doing."* A bunch of photos of mostly uneaten and sloppy piles of expensive cheese at the end of an event opens everyone up to a different kind of conversation, including recommendations to make charcuterie more appealing and easier to serve for guests.

If we're in it all together, then no one person is in trouble and it's easier for everyone to see past the mistakes and get down to solving the problem.

MAKE IT TACTILE!

Providing teams with visceral experiences is potent! Diana used a real-life approach in a practical way. "When we were trying to change to more energy efficient light bulbs, I went out and bought different options and did some testing in hallways. I did surveys in person with staff in different departments. I even talked to customers and asked how they felt about certain lighting. The general manager came by one of the areas while I was testing and when he saw the light, he was on board!"

Jack took the cigarette butt visual one step further. He wanted to connect a group with aspects of the environment they weren't typically seeing or thinking about. "I organized litter cleanups. I thought it would be a good way to get our software engineers to think about the environment. They get so comfortable being on the computer, but I wanted to get them out of their office chair, take them outside to pick up litter. They always leave understanding there's so many intricate things thrown everywhere, and it's a mess. Walking the grounds is an easy thing to do. It's not anything revolutionary."

Experience sparks empathy. Researchers found through experiments with virtual reality (VR) they were able to illicit empathy for the future state of coral reefs when they gave participants an opportunity to *"swim"* among both healthy and devastated reefs.[3] Despite my frequent warnings to stay positive, and to support the notion that there is a time and place for alarmist content, they found the devastated reef garnered more empathy. This research also found empathy in any learning scenario (VR or non-VR) dissipated greatly after three months, reinforcing the principle of repetition as an important part of the overall enlightenment strategy.[4]

To take this hands-on approach a step further, I recommend piloting initiatives anytime remotely feasible. Prove you can do it once and show its effectiveness, and then it's easier to make it a permanent change. In some cases, especially when nuanced engineering or design is involved, set up options and ask people to vote or compare and contrast a before and after scenario.

This is helpful with something as convoluted as recycling. The entropy of garbage makes recycling a massive pain in the butt. So many different types of materials and even the most detailed signage over a recycling bin can leave people confused. If you test different colors, icons, messages, and let people give feedback, you are likely to uncover solutions no one had thought of.

I recently visited a client site where we walked multiple docks throughout the campus. A problem they faced was the docks were not set up in a way conducive to efficient waste management. We designed an activity to bring cross-functional teams onto the docks with sidewalk chalk and flip charts to mock-up directional paint and signage. It's easy to be blasé about things when you do not personally have to deal with the consequences, so this type of activity makes everyone aware of their part in the chain of action leading to waste streams.

Ask for volunteers to help sort recycling. Yes, it's a dirty job, but if you can offer an incentive to get people to put some gloved hands in the trash, they will have a whole different appreciation for how much trouble their little recycling sins cause. For example, if you want to institute a compost program in an office breakroom requiring people to first scrape food off their plate into one bin and then put plastic into a separate bin, you are likely to find people will throw all sorts of other things into the compost—forks, napkins, muffin wrappers, whatever.

It's easy for people to think it doesn't matter or that they aren't part of the problem. If you gamify this experience among departments and various breakrooms, the consequence of an individual's apathy becomes readily apparent.

At one convention center, the team set up a partnership with a local pig farmer. Due to state regulations and farmer preferences, only certain types of scraps could go into the pig farm bin. Line cooks and stewards got careless. They were not connecting the fact that pigs do not eat plastic wrap, hairnets, and other things thrown in with the pig feed. Take those people out to visit the farm and send around photos of newborn piglets, and suddenly the mentality and care are there.

DON'T LET ANYONE DIM YOUR LIGHT

A final note on this theme. Some people simply will not be enlightened. They literally do not care. They may be bitter, inconvenienced, or just plain assholes! You can't wake a person pretending to sleep.

Don't beat yourself up if even your best attempts at enlightenment fail with certain people. In fact, you may find a bit of a bell curve in your attempts to message sustainability. People who don't or won't care at all take up one end of the spectrum. Most people are mildly intrigued and at least somewhat informed. They sit in the middle. Those who are sparked, excited, and ready to move rest at the other end of the spectrum. Pour your energy into them! Do not waste your heart or efforts on converting doubters. Consider and acknowledge them as their stakeholder type demands, but do not judge *your* success on *their* response.

I often remind myself when speaking to a room of people that if even one person changes how they think or act on this topic, I will have done a marvelous thing. Eventually, for sustainability to succeed and spread, you'll need more than one person, but if you doubt the power of one person's passion, view a TED Talk by Derek Sivers called "How to Start a Movement."[5] It's a funny and powerful reminder that our efforts will be rewarded if we persist.

EXPONENTIAL IMPACT APPLICATION AND DISCUSSION

- Learn the language: on a whiteboard, write the core concept you are trying to push within your organization. Then write the words your audience or stakeholders might better recognize when this topic comes up.

- Create a mood board for your initiative to identify potential visuals that will resonate.

- What field trips would impact your key audience to change their attitude and behaviors? For example, waste management companies offer tours of their materials recovery facilities (MRFs). Regenerative farmers love to share what they're doing, and new buildings may allow access to their rooftop beehives and solar panels. Seeing these things up close and personal is a game changer.

- Apply the PEACE framework described in this chapter to a current or planned sustainability communication or education plan.

PART 3:

EMPOWER

CHAPTER 15

EMPOWER: WALK THE TALK

EMPOWERMENT IS THE CORNERSTONE

Empowerment is letting the genie out of the bottle! We need environments where desire, passion, energy, and creativity can manifest into action.

Empowerment is a common thread across every champion's story. It's the cornerstone because everything ultimately hinges on it. All the engagement principles in this book work together. In the way empathy builds a solid foundation, all the principles are stronger and more powerful when coupled with empowerment.

When management listens and practices empathy but doesn't authorize action, the initiative is decoration only. If leaders raise awareness but do not allow people to follow through on this inspiring new information, the messages ring hollow. Companies can install the necessary systems and equip everybody through training, but if staff doesn't feel empowered to make decisions and troubleshoot problems, those systems fail.

Empowerment goes hand in hand with autonomy and trust—two critical job characteristics sustainability champions I speak with crave. When people don't have autonomy, it's like being a robot in a job. Why am I even here if I can't add value with my own personal stamp? The champion craves meaning but if not equipped and sanctioned to act, that desire remains trapped inside and becomes a lost opportunity. Autonomy comes about either because someone in the organization extends it to the champion or because the champion sees what they want and goes for it. In the best-case scenario, it's both.

Diana's nearly twenty-year career in sustainability started as an excellent example of what happens when a self-determined person enters the scene. "My sustainability career started by accident. I was taking a class in sustainable tourism. A professor suggested if we liked this topic to start somewhere and start now. At the time I was a front desk agent at a hotel and saw opportunities to be more sustainable. I went to the GM and proposed we start a green team. He told me he was waiting for the right person to raise their hand and I came to him at the right time."

Diana continued, "A few years later, I was at a different hotel and I raised my hand again and offered to start a sustainability committee. When the recession hit and my colleagues in sales lost their jobs, the GM proposed I do sustainability full-time. No one in that whole company had ever had that title, but he saw it as important."

ACTIVATE PASSION

For some, this ability to forge a new pathway is formidable—either because the obstacles are too great or, more likely, they tend to be passive in their jobs. They have interest, maybe even passion, but are waiting for permission to do anything with it. In these cases, it won't take much to get the champion going but they do need a boost.

I delivered training to a team of about seventy-five people who worked for a global corporation with an award-winning sustainability program; however, the sustainability knowledge in the room was low. Their application of it in their jobs was just about nil. At the end of the session, I displayed a poll asking how many would be interested in having or being on a committee that meets to discuss how to best address the topic with their clients. The majority responded in the positive.

I also asked how many would be interested in being a subject matter expert who could be called upon to support others in this area. Almost thirty percent of the respondents said they would! While my workshop enabled many to embark on a learning journey, it did not serve as an official mechanism for these people to say *"sign me up."* Executives must formalize these intentions through programs and tasks. Activate these people, and you've got exponential impact!

When organizational leaders instill even a little bit of confidence and give the green light, those with the drive can champion causes and change. These situations require a more intentional approach because the prevalent scenario is passionate volunteers operating in an informal capacity. At this stage, sustainability looks like a bolt-on to other things, and the initiatives are still somewhat unofficial.

Once traction kicks in and a few more converts have joined the cause, enabling sustainability morphs to a more official and formal endeavor. Interestingly, I find in many cases a similar path whereby some impetus drives what would normally be an ambitious undertaking before a truly developed sustainability program is launched. Policies precede strategy. Reporting precedes results. Certification precedes integration.

A strong will pushes the team through the extreme challenges of achieving these objectives. Customer or market demand or a powerful external force, such as new regulations, serve as the stimulus. Per an earlier chapter, consultants are commonly brought in at this stage and because these deliverables—setting policy, measurement and reporting, and certifying to a set of standards—are sufficiently detailed and comprehensive, it drives rapid adoption of new practices and assignment of resources.

Eventually, in this chicken and egg progression, the organizational leaders acquiesce sustainability is here to stay and begin to value its role by setting strategic goals and measuring overall performance. One might think this is where empowerment becomes part of the culture, but one might be wrong. Too often, the inertia of the prevailing dynamic is too strong.

Lior Arussy brilliantly contrasted organizations with and without this powerful force in an article in Chief Executive Magazine. "With empowerment, organizations are agile..., fast-moving, and living by their purpose. That means they empower the right employees to make the right decisions at the moment of truth. Without it, they are towers of ancient silos—deploying old weaponry, protected by feudal and conflicting executive agendas that have a patina of collaboration, which does not last beyond the short-lived, fake smiles of their leadership meetings."[1]

He also argues a point I consistently remind clients: not empowering and involving all staff makes it more likely they will not only not comply with initiatives, but they may actively sabotage them. Arussy stated about one organization his firm assessed, "Too many people held the power to stop, delay, and otherwise avoid new initiatives..."[2]

In global corporations, the real danger is when headquarters announces and touts initiatives, but at the operational level, employees are not walking the talk. This leads to greenwashing.

Without a concerted effort to delegate staff from top to bottom, successful or impactful social and environmental programs can be limited. Here, sustainability needs to be designed and programmed into corporate mechanisms and embedded into the culture.

Empowerment happens in stages and will be expounded upon in the following chapters:

- **Agency and Autonomy** is a recurring theme when the champion or small group of champions volunteers themselves and happens to be in an environment where that is accepted. Agency and autonomy spark truly transformational change but can also create chaos because those champions are prone to break rules along the way.

- **Activation** is needed because those who are not likely to raise their hand and volunteer, but very much want to be involved, need a strong nudge. We must be willing to perceive the vein of gold in the mountain. If agency is a well bursting forth, activation taps the well of enthusiasm lying beneath the surface, extracting energy, and providing outlets for action.

- **Acceleration** happens when eventually others in the organization realize, *"oh, this is a thing, we actually have work to do."* Here we equip the champion or green team to carry out programs and grant them official authority. Sustainability is enabled through adjustments in resource allocation and pursuit of standards.

- **Actualization** is when sustainability is ingrained in the very DNA of the organization. Social and environmental impact is assimilated via strategy, goal setting, standard operating procedures, job descriptions, and any number of typical corporate mechanisms.

EXPONENTIAL IMPACT APPLICATION AND DISCUSSION

- As a sustainability champion, in what way do you feel you have approval to act?

- In what ways are you waiting for permission to bring forth social or environmental initiatives? How does that stall sustainability programs for you or others in your organization? How does that impact you personally in your career?

- In what ways are executives overlooking the power of some in the organization to diminish or sabotage results because they have not been suitably empowered? Conversely, looking at initiatives other than sustainability, in what ways have the organization's leadership allowed staff to support the initiative so it thrives?

CHAPTER 16

AGENCY AND AUTONOMY: CHAMPIONS RISE UP

RECIPE FOR CHAMPIONS

True changemakers are those willing to step into unknown territory and take big leaps with no safety net. Sometimes they come up with the idea and make it happen with sheer will. Other times they are voluntold because someone saw something special in them (or just threw them in the deep end to avoid diving in themselves).

These employees have a great deal of agency. They drive change in a way that creates opportunities for others to take action. They are divided between what is their actual job and this other thing they'd probably prefer to spend their day doing. Without a formal job description or department, what rules should they adhere to? What assurance do they have their work will be acknowledged, much less rewarded? Not acting is not an option so they try and, even if they fail, the trying makes them feel alive.

The concept of agency is that someone has control over their own life, with higher levels of independence, assertiveness, tenacity, and risk tolerance than most have. A sense of destiny drives the high agency person. This person knows they can make a difference; they *must* make a difference.

> *"A sense of destiny drives the high agency person. This person knows they can make a difference; they must make a difference."*

We recognize these people in general as they tend to be achievers and leaders, but these characteristics in the context of sustainability are the spark to ignite the engine when the organization is earlier on the journey. Remember, in this phase, little to no formal sustainability is happening, so these champions must blaze a new trail, which inevitably comes with thorns. It's helpful these people are not afraid of a few cuts and bruises if that's what it takes to reach the summit.

In practical real-life terms, this plays out in several ways. I'll start with my own story. My trajectory was very much *"fake it 'til you make it"*! One of the first steps any of these champions must take is to sell someone on their idea. The internal champions have a tough time, but when you're an outsider, forget about it! It's challenging for many who start their own consulting firms to go from the doer to the seller. We get into the work because we want to change the world, not because we want to create brochures or figure out how much to charge for our time.

My vision and desire was strong enough I had to figure out how to get over that hump. I followed my own advice to students for years, which was to find small projects to do for free to build their résumé. Once I proved to myself I could do it and add value, I was able to speak much more confidently to others about my services.

Cheryl is a young professional I spoke with about her champion experience. She landed a marketing role because a friend worked at the hiring company. Her path was more a question of what's the first door to open at such an early point in a somewhat directionless career. People who take the route of experimentation and indecisiveness early on don't always know what they're looking for but know it when they see it.

Cheryl described how she made the most of the opportunity. "On my first day, I looked around and was like, 'What am I doing here? I don't know anything about marketing.' I enjoyed the process of learning about digital marketing and enhancing my communication skills. Then I took it upon myself to become a green team leader, which was me once again stepping into a role where I didn't know what I was doing. I was going to throw stuff at the wall and see what happened. I was able to introduce and sell coworkers on a plastic straw ban and other waste-reduction initiatives."

Sarah also entered through the marketing door, but like many champions, her route was not straightforward. She had to take leaps and expose herself in a way many are not willing to do. She described her path of action.

"I went to school for a general BA and quickly fell in love with environmental studies. But when I got out of school, I couldn't find a job, so I ended up blogging about cleaning up litter along my running route. I got the community involved. There was a snapshot of me shared on television, so I got attention from the mayor. I was just sitting around applying for jobs, feeling helpless, honestly, so I picked up litter. I started to understand how sharing it ripples out and other people feel inspired to do the same."

Sarah connected her environmental interest with the role of marketing to spread messages and inspire others. The importance of this is how often I hear young people express frustration that their title or job function does not officially include sustainability. Staff with agency take it upon themselves to make sustainability their job within the context of what their job already is officially.

Even those champions with the greatest agency require an environment of trust, with a degree of autonomy. To read some business management headlines, it's easy to sense a fundamental shift in corporate environments. Conventional assumptions often dictate how people should be managed and productivity imposed.

Coming out of COVID, executives have grappled with restoring a sense of control after a season of flexibility had prevailed. Employees aren't having it. A study by Korn Ferry showed 72 percent would choose a lower salary if it meant being able to work from home, 58 percent indicated they would experience negative mental health consequences if required to go back to the office, and more than 90 percent felt their manager cares more about whether the employee is in the office than they do the employee themselves.[1]

There is something to be said for in-person interaction and the opportunity to observe work and build relationships; however, such a move should not be perceived as removing choice, freedom, or autonomy. This sends a message employees cannot be trusted to do their work. Does this sound conducive to innovation and bringing forth new ideas for positive impact?

MANAGE THE PERSON, NOT THE TASK

Successful sustainability initiatives generally mean someone behind them is passionate, self-motivated, productive, and ready for more. Who wouldn't want employees like that throughout their organization? Unfortunately, all too often, the enthusiasm and efforts of such people are squelched because they operate in unknown territory and those around and above them, who are ego-driven and need to be in control, are threatened by this energy.

When managers do not understand new concepts introduced into their business, self-preservation kicks in, which causes many to exercise poor management and drive away the employees most needed to move the needle in social and environmental programs.

A perfect example of both the right and wrong way to approach this is in Jana's story. I first met her when she hosted a gathering to promote sustainability in her city and industry. It was an excellent event, and I was drawn to her enthusiasm for the topic. We stayed in touch, and I have learned more about what she does and how she has done it.

Jana is like many women of her generation—younger than I am but not young enough to have been born into a world where girls are taught very early it's okay to be a total badass. She did not recognize how what she had accomplished was special or different.

Jana's start in sustainability was the ultimate approach to empowerment that's frequently a hallmark of the sustainability journey. She was voluntold to run sustainability at her facility, which included a stadium, event space, warehouse, and retail. The complexity of the facility made this surprise assignment even more ambitious. In fact, this decision wasn't even communicated directly to her (probably because no one had the guts to tell her to her face what she'd been signed up for!). Thanks to happenstance, she found out in an elevator when someone congratulated her. She had no idea what for.

It isn't as uncommon as you might think that an unsuspecting staffer is assigned such an important role. This stems from sustainability still being an unknown and managers knowing they need to address it, but even they don't know what that entails.

In the next chapter, this thread continues; someone is nudged into the position rather than claim it for themselves from the beginning. The difference is those with high agency and a strong sense of direction need less support and, as we see in Jana's story, more autonomy.

Jana met the challenge and successfully implemented sustainability initiatives. She single-handedly recruited and ran a green team spanning different businesses under one roof. She sought knowledge and upskilling by attending webinars and events. She tested different options for each problem.

Fast forward a couple of years and Jana left that job. It's only in hindsight she realized what she had at the time she was accomplishing that greatness. "I reported to the VP of Operations, and he allowed me a level of autonomy employees dream about. You know, he was like, 'Just as long as it gets done and nothing negative comes across my desk, I don't care.' He supported my development and told me to go study this, go earn this certification, go to this conference, do this tour, do whatever the clients like. Sometimes I had to chase him around to tell him what I was doing!"

Some might argue that's too much autonomy but it's better than the other end of the spectrum. Unfortunately, that empowering boss retired, and in his place stepped a control freak. Jana ended up resigning from this job she had been in for a decade. Like many who are ready to move on, she no longer felt empowered. She felt micromanaged. Jana explained situations where her past knowledge, experience, and connections would have made a big difference, but her recommendations were consistently batted down and her ideas ignored.

She continued, "No, I wasn't supposed to ask questions. I was supposed to just do it. Okay, got it, no problem. Consider it done. I mean, if you don't choose to use my ideas, that's fine, but hear me out. I didn't work all these years in all these facilities for nothing. Just support me, you know. I know that autonomy my previous employer gave me has to be earned. I respect that. But let me get there."

Jana's experience of going from empowered to controlled negatively impacts an employee's psyche and motivation. Regrettably, too many feel forced to put up with it, but everyone has their breaking point. She said, "It got to a point where I didn't feel they deserved my efforts anymore. Like all the blood, sweat, tears, and lack of sleep and energy I'd given to this didn't matter. I hit a wall."

What stands out most to me was Jana's comment "manage the person, not the task." She felt micromanaged, and for the person with high agency, that is putting a tiger in a cage! One study showed 79 percent of surveyed employees have experienced micromanagement and 71 percent said it interfered with their job. Astonishingly, 85 percent claimed a negative impact to their morale and for 69 percent it led them to consider leaving their job.[2]

In his book *My Way or the Highway: The Micromanagement Survival Guide*, Harry Chambers describes characteristics of this detrimental management style. Tendencies like control, manipulation, power imbalances, unnecessary steps and approvals, hovering, dismissing, and disrespect are indicative of micromanagement.[3] Anyone who has ever been a manager understands the fine line you must walk to get the results and output needed while allowing people to take longer than it would if you were doing the job, or not be as perfect as you might like it or done in a different way.

When I was micromanaged, which is just about the worst thing you could do to me, I ended up feeling my supervisor didn't trust me or have faith I could do the job well. My self-confidence took a hit. I got defensive, protective really, of myself. That's no way to be if you're trying to promote a positive environment for customers and colleagues. It was toxic, even traumatic.

Like Jana, I had the benefit of a hands-off boss early in my career. My first job as a database programmer was an internship in my computer information systems undergraduate program. The first day I was shown a program and given high-level instructions on what it was supposed to do. I remember thinking, *"Uh, do they know I don't know how to code yet?"* I took the manual home and read it over the weekend and started coding the next week. While I've always been proud of this ability, I don't know if I appreciated how pivotal that would be to how my career would play out. This was the first of a few empowering managers I had over the years. I owe a lot to them for those moments of trust.

I was thrilled to hear Jana's journey took her to a place where she recognized the value of her work. She also gives back by mentoring others. For a variety of reasons, many employees may not leave a miserable situation. They are stuck and need a Jana or Aurora to illuminate a path. I know a significant factor in new generations of champions having the courage to forge ahead is the inspiration of people like us who share our hearts, time, and encouragement with others to spur them on. In fact, it was early in the journey of starting my company I attended the event Jana organized. I can speak from personal experience that her endurance mattered!

EXPONENTIAL IMPACT APPLICATION AND DISCUSSION

- As a leader, ponder the following:

    o   Who among your staff has agency to go after the tough social and environmental challenges of your organization?

    o   Have you denied your staff autonomy through micromanagement?

    o   In what ways can you show trust and provide autonomy to potential or active champions? Consider low-risk, high-reward initiatives they can take charge of or pilot.

- As a young champion or wannabe sustainability professional, ask yourself:

  o Have you taken action demonstrating to others both your passion and ability to drive change?

  o In what ways have you taken charge of your career direction and work tasks? What opportunities remain for you to empower yourself to step into roles and assignments you desire?

CHAPTER 17

ACTIVATION: RALLY THE TROOPS

POWERLESS VORTEX

Charlotte worked in the customer service department of a regional bank. She arrived at work and on the way to her desk she saw a familiar yet infuriating sight: trash in the recycle bin. More specifically, a plastic grocery bag and a banana peel were comingled with soda cans and water bottles. Charlotte had been proud when her company installed the recycle bins, but it seemed like no one used them properly and no one in leadership seemed to care.

She had even observed executives patting themselves on the back for their environmental measures. At the last company town hall, the CEO bragged, "All our offices are now participating in our robust recycling program, and we have set a goal to be zero waste by 2035!"

Recycling is only one of the lackluster sustainability initiatives Charlotte noticed. The company still has not made any effort in many areas of sustainability. She felt the disconnect between executive claims and her daily reality.

When Charlotte got to her computer, she checked a weekly industry newsletter and learned a competitor had just published an annual sustainability report. She felt even more let down that her firm's leadership made promises with no system of reporting or accountability.

Charlotte's sense of powerlessness added to her aggravation. With no one in charge of sustainability for the company, Charlotte did not know where to turn. She constantly thought of looking for a job with a company that shared her ethos for the environment. She checked that competitor's website to seek openings and indeed a position for an entry-level role in the sustainability department appeared in the list. Charlotte read the required qualifications and felt instantly depressed. The job description read, "Must have a degree in environmental science." The thought of going back to college and accumulating more student loan debt was less appealing than working for a company with fake sustainability messaging.

Charlotte trudged through the rest of the day and felt less and less energy for her work. Her disappointment prevented her from being the bright spot of the department she normally was. Her coworkers picked up on this malaise and became concerned. While Charlotte may have been discouraged, she was too invested in a better world to sit idly by. What would prompt a change? Where would Charlotte find the courage to act?

Many people like Charlotte want purpose in their careers, but they assume a special title or education is the only pathway to work in sustainability. The sad reality is they see it as an exclusive or unreachable position. They wait for permission to live out their dreams of making a difference. This empty space in their professional desires can become a black hole in which energy and passion for the job overall are sucked in and likely never to be recovered.

Earlier, I presented the findings of the 2023 Gallup research on workplace engagement, which is derived from a survey of more than 15,000 US employees and shows employee engagement dropping. According to Gallup, even those who are "actively disengaged," meaning they tend to make the workplace miserable for those around them and sap productivity out of teams, was increasing.[1]

The Gallup research also revealed two of the top three contributors to that decline in employee engagement included employees not feeling connected to the mission or purpose of the company or to opportunities for development. Among those surveyed, the younger age groups had greater declines in engagement and increases in active disengagement.[2]

This is echoed in a study by LHH, a talent advisory firm, in which they investigated how people feel about the future and their level of readiness to adapt to change and evolve in the workplace. One of the drivers exposed in this research was "a culture that promotes people and makes them feel that they have a promising pathway."[3] The 18 to 24 age group felt more anxious about their next career move and one third thought their voice wasn't heard compared to older people.[4] They also tended to not have good relationships with their work peers.[5] Overall, 75 percent wanted a change in their career.[6]

When Charlotte and others like her spend their day thinking about greener grass somewhere else, that makes them miserable. It's no wonder they are not developing healthy and productive relationships with coworkers. They want a career move, but that does not mean it has to happen outside the walls of their current job.

It's not realistic in most organizations to instantly create sustainability positions and ask people to raise their hands. The journey starts with more of a grassroots origin, with conversations in the break room about recycling or, more likely, criticisms spoken in the break room about **not** recycling. That talk can quickly become negative and futile.

Alternatively, you can foster a safe space where chatter becomes opportunity. Empower staff to make decisions and choices with low risk and low cost. I have toured many a kitchen where a brilliant solution for recycling came from a line cook or dishwasher who felt empowered to share an idea. Because many sustainability initiatives do not have one-size-fits-all solutions, those within the organization, who care about what happens there, can be creative and formulate customized solutions.

TWO DOORS, SAME ROOM

Ideally, the Charlottes of the world would be empowered to suggest ideas, design initiatives, and be a leader among their peers. What does it look like to empower a Charlotte? Don't overthink it. Sometimes it's just cracking a door and welcoming someone inside.

Later that day, Charlotte went to the break room and saw more trash in the recycling bin. She grumbled underneath her breath and started picking garbage out of bins and separating it. Behind her a voice asked, "What are you doing?"

Surprised, Charlotte turned around and was face-to-face with the CEO! She couldn't back out, so she timidly explained sometimes people put the wrong items in the recycle bins.

Fortunately for Charlotte, this was a CEO who cared. He asked her more questions about recycling and put her at ease. After a few minutes, Charlotte had unloaded her frustrations and sat wondering *"now what?"* The CEO asked if she would be interested in running a small task force to improve break room recycling. Charlotte was delighted, empowered, filled with purpose and excitement to solve this problem. The light was once again shining in her department.

Over the past decade of having conversations with college students and young professionals, I have observed most who are trying to find their way into some area of sustainability start in another role. In fact, until the last couple of years when the sustainability field has exploded in growth, it was extremely rare I encountered someone who started their tenure in a sustainability capacity.

For many, this means incongruity pervades their career experience. Social and environmental causes, or purpose-driven work in general, is another dimension they need to feel whole. Before they figure out how a functional career choice relates to any cause, their daily efforts may feel meaningless.

Two primary paths emerge for these young people. One is they are natural go-getters and rather self-aware. When an individual knows who they are, what they bring to the table, what their passion is, and what their gifts are, this enables them to find, or create, a role compatible with who they are. They raise their hand and say *"yes"* to whatever it takes. We met these people in the last chapter.

The other primary path is one I've seen play out more often. In the years I spent in higher education, I taught first generation college students, immigrants, and inner-city residents who had rarely ventured far from their neighborhoods. Perhaps because of systemic racism in our society or because they lacked the parental or educational nudging to stand out in the crowd, most of these students and young professionals were sitting on the sidelines waiting to get called into the game.

The passion and talent trapped in them is a treasure trove! Mentors and pathways are needed to extract it. This person may not self-identify as the champion. They need a persuasive and generous person to prod them. I taught a college class where starting a green team at their workplace (or church, dorm, or neighborhood) was compulsory. I gave them a blueprint to follow.

I only required they start a team. I reminded them a team can consist of only two people because I figured they could convince at least one coworker to join. I did not expect them to make actual changes, or at least not for their grade. I could not guarantee they could instigate operational upgrades in their workplaces.

Whoa, did I underestimate them! Over the years, I saw students implement everything from having toilets replaced to eliminating plastic water bottles, from organizing beach cleanups to convincing bosses to install electric vehicle charging stations (before that was the rage it is now).

I have known many Charlottes in years of teaching and mentoring. When I hear their stories, I hear the transformation happening in their workplaces through these small examples of empowerment. As a teacher, I was often the one enabling until they found their voice and had the courage to speak up to bosses. Most of the time, once the manager saw the potential, they picked up the empowerment cue and fostered even greater self-assurance and growth.

At times, both students and I were let down over brilliant ideas dying on the vine, which is indicative of an overall culture issue that leaders have failed to or refuse to remedy. Hence, we see the dismal results of Gallup's US employee engagement study referenced earlier.

"Empowerment converts desire into innovation and productivity."

Those changemakers who successfully overcame obstacles and forged paths of change and leadership are ones we end up seeing on the news, like the fifteen-year-old who led a climate march that shocked a city.[7] Those are the exceptions to the rule; most young people have potential in them, even if they don't make headlines. Empowerment converts desire into innovation and productivity.

If you are able to spark one of them, do yourself and them a favor and make that happen. Two of the best ways to stimulate the hidden champion are education and pilots.

EMPOWERMENT MECHANISMS

EDUCATION

As noted previously, I do not subscribe to the idea one must have an environmental degree to embark on a sustainability career. Numerous options exist for educating champions without the expense or time required for a full degree—credentials, certificate programs, conference sessions, webinars, etc.

Many champions, including myself, got our start by consuming as many of these options as we could. We initiated action because we felt compelled to apply what we were discovering about social and environmental issues and advancements. When people learn, they naturally feel more inclined to practice their new skills and apply their new knowledge.

When I was studying for two sustainability credentials in 2016, I loved connecting the new words and concepts I was learning with what I was seeing in the world or reading in sustainability news. One of those, the LEED Green Associate, is from the US Green Building Council. I had never known much about the built environment so anytime I saw evidence of the things I was learning (for example, energy efficiency, stormwater management, air quality improvements), I felt so validated for the time I was investing.

Even though I was still a novice, I couldn't wait to utilize this awareness in a client project. I was never going to be the consultant advising on these technical topics, but I knew I needed to hold my own in a conversation with a building engineer. My plan was always to be the change management and employee engagement expert, but to do that I needed to speak the language of the operational folks. I couldn't wait to take my new vocabulary out for a spin. I attended networking events and felt proud I could ask intelligent questions of a panel or make observations about the sustainability benefits of new regulations.

It's important for the potential champion to have opportunities to study topics that will enhance their confidence and credibility. Since sustainability education is not typically on the radar of corporate human resources or learning and development teams; start with external programs. Ideally, enable employees to earn credentials they might leverage throughout their career.

David's experience exemplifies this. He did not have a background in sustainability when he started working at a convention center but found targeted sustainability education beneficial. In his case, his employer's investment in his education paid dividends when David was there and as he moved through his career in subsequent positions within the center's ecosystem. "I started on the ground and worked my way up. I was the custodial manager and just handled trash. Because of the certification the company was going for, I needed credentials too, so I became a LEED AP. I also got my Sustainable Event Professional Certificate. Now I am the sustainability manager at one of the vendors I used to work with at the center."

I'd like to point out how David stated he was *"just"* the guy who handled trash. Note how people downplay the importance of their part and the value they add when their role is only operational. Also, David probably could have opted for the same certification I got, the

LEED Green Associate, which is an entry-level option. David went for the AP, which is substantially more advanced. Education can set off a chain reaction of self-improvement and confidence in the right champions.

The number of sustainability programs at the university level, as well as certificate courses, has exploded in recent years. Most industry associations now offer education on relevant social and environmental topics, ranging from short webinars to official credentials. Media companies, such as GreenBiz and Sustainable Brands, focus solely on social and environmental topics and offer regular education through virtual sessions and in-person conferences.

Carve out budget to offer sustainability education. Signing up for a short course is a safe move for staff and an excellent way for executives to spot those interested in sustainability who would otherwise have gone unnoticed.

PILOT PROJECTS

A slightly riskier, but still innocuous, approach to empowering staff is to pilot initiatives and allow experimentation with new approaches. Better yet, identify someone with leadership potential and put them in charge of the pilot. Those with agency and autonomy will likely come up with ideas, but for those who need a safer start, give them the context and boundaries (for example, budget, timeline).

Think of a pilot as anything you either do on a temporary basis or within a limited area of operations. You can try something once just to see what insights and improvements can be gleaned without the commitment to an ongoing lift of this nature.

I had a convention center client with a great deal of waste management efforts underway, but we identified missed opportunities. Installing new dumpsters and equipment was out of the question until a future budget cycle, so we sought ways to improve existing programs. I recommended they pilot an e-waste collection program for exhibitors and contractors. This existed for the office, but we heard it was spotty at best. We had noticed lots of cables in the dumpsters near exhibit halls, so we knew there was no effort happening there.

We determined we could do a pilot with a minimal investment in collection containers and temporary signage. We started with a small trade show, so all involved got to safely try something out with little risk and low expectations. We figured out the logistics on a small scale so they would be able to roll it out with greater certainty later at a larger show. This pilot resulted in gathering more e-waste than we could have imagined, proving to decision makers this is an undertaking worth expanding.

The timing of this pilot coincided with the start of a new sustainability manager. The person who stepped in the role had amazing leadership skills and industry experience, but a pilot afforded her the opportunity to get to know the players, the building infrastructure, the contracts, and other details at a digestible pace. More importantly, it allowed other staff who had been disengaged or even discouraged on the topic of waste to see that change was coming and that this person had what it took to drive that change. This built trust and momentum for all involved.

EXPONENTIAL IMPACT APPLICATION AND DISCUSSION

- What steps have been taken in your organization to identify the Charlottes? What opportunities do they have to express interest or be empowered to drive change?

- Work with department leaders to identify existing sustainability initiatives where the performance is lackluster and needs a redesign or fresh infusion of energy and ideas. Assign the green team or the Charlottes of the organization the task of improving these programs. Resist the temptation to only allow those within a department to solve that department's problems. Cross-functional teams deepen the activation as staff discover interests and abilities to serve they didn't know were in them.

- To perform the activity above, you may find you first have to overcome some *"we're good here"* mentalities. When I work virtually with clients because they don't make room in the budget for travel, I have to take their word for what's going well and what's a problem. Mostly, I hear the thing I'm asking about isn't a problem. That's pretty much never true. Contrast that to the client experiences where I'm allowed to walk around and take photos of trash cans and talk to random staff I encounter. It's night and day.

Don't be afraid to poke your head in areas you might not normally enter; that's how you ascertain what's really going on. Work with the green team to inventory the opportunities; an outside consultant might be helpful in this because it matters less if they step on a few toes. Set the tone that this does not mean people are in trouble. Reassure everyone this is an exercise in continuous improvement. Take lots of photos! Ask lots of questions!

CHAPTER 18

ACCELERATION: SPEEDING UP SUSTAINABILITY

LET OTHERS DRIVE

My dad has always been a fast car kind of guy and from time to time he takes me out to show off his latest speed toy or let me have my turn at the wheel. He let me drive his souped-up Cadillac down a country road (this thing was so badass it came with a weekend-long high-performance driving school!). I was timidly driving about sixty miles an hour. He told me, "Step on it." I did, and holy crap, Batman! That car reached almost a hundred miles an hour in no time flat. As much as I love to go fast, it freaked me out, and I immediately backed off.

When things in life start to accelerate, it's exhilarating but scary. Once you've acclimated to the speed, you're ready to find that next gear. This is true of champions who start and drive sustainability in organizations. What many of them learn along the way is, at some point, they have to take their hands off the wheel and let others drive. To go faster, you might first have to slow down.

I'm terribly impatient, but I've learned to appreciate and respect the natural evolution of sustainability in an organization or within divisions of a larger entity. I've witnessed the transformation when companies hit a critical mass and begin to move more rapidly toward exponential impact, when the movement goes from the lone volunteer everyone rolls their eyes at to a sanctioned green team and official initiatives.

A green team, or whatever you want to call the sustainability committee, task force, or employee resource group, is vital and for so long was underutilized. When I first got into sustainability, I heard time and again responses to the idea of a green team along the lines of *"been there, done that."* The general mentality toward sustainability is somehow it's a *"one-and-done"* thing. Is that how we approach marketing or finance? We *had* a team so we're good. No! It's ongoing.

A green team extends the span of control from one person pushing the boulder up the hill by providing reach, buy-in, and insights from other domains of the organization. It makes driving change safer and sustainability more formal yet still not entirely integrated or actualized across the company.

For the person who started this movement, this is an interesting time of growth. Chance, whom I introduced you to earlier, reflected on his experience. "I think it was still too reliant upon me. I was this galvanizing force. I was the one always moving it to the next step, bridging the gap between staff and leadership or this organization and that organization, and it's a lot for one person."

Chance described a turning point with his team. "I knew we'd achieved an empowerment shift when I'd go to our general manager with ideas and he would ask, 'Well, what does the green team think? Have you guys voted on this?' I'm like, yeah, we have, and here are our recommendations. The GM would respond, 'If they want to do it, let's do it, we'll figure it out.' A housekeeper or an engineer felt comfortable bringing ideas to us. They knew they were going to get support, and it was like a rocket ship through the sky."

When the green team itself has agency, sustainability picks up speed. Some launch surreptitiously and grow organically. They exist because an executive didn't say no and the champion could take their pet project to the next level. One of my former students experienced this. Since her course assignment was to start a green team, the hotel general manager gave her the *"sure, why not"* nod of approval. Then weeks later, he noticed people were showing up to the meetings. He saw a shift in the culture and nearby competitors were taking note! That's when he personally took interest and began to proactively support the team.

Distributed participation and dispersed leadership are paramount for effective sustainability programs. That's how it grows exponentially. It might be a bit messy at first, but the dynamics of these conversations reverberate an energy throughout the organization and momentum bubbles underneath the surface. Change starts brewing.

"Distributed participation and dispersed leadership are paramount for effective sustainability programs."

As we get into this phase, all involved begin to acknowledge it as a real responsibility. What might have been this weird faction of people thought of as tree huggers now controls something kind of critical. This recognition chips away at organizational apathy and helps the team internalize they have both the duty and power to change the status quo.

It's about creating space for people to explore, suggest, question, and experiment. When I'm in these rooms, I carry a lot of weight and, because I know so much and am viewed as an expert, this can be intimidating. I provide recommendations and people view them almost as recipes to follow precisely, if not rules that must be obeyed. I remind them, "These are my proposals, but what resonates with *you*? It's okay if you only choose to accept one out of one hundred. You can come up with your own that are not on my list. It has to feel right for you and your team."

KEEP UP THE MOMENTUM

Once the green team gains speed, it's time to further formalize and reinforce sustainability, which at this point is *"official, not official."* What does it take to make it official? In addition to a green team, trigger points kick in more substantial momentum. These include:

- Policies

- Pledges

- Positions

POLICIES

Sustainability finds a new gear when the green team commences drafting policies. For many sustainability certification schemes, policies on key social and environmental issues are foundational and mandatory. Certifying bodies are not super prescriptive because they accommodate a wide range of organizations and scenarios. For example, you may be required to have a policy on green cleaning but what is in that policy may be open to interpretation. The policy can range from a high-level statement about purchasing eco-labeled products to fine-tooth comb detail about accepted formulas and practices.

A criticism of policies is they seem to have no teeth or create loopholes and exceptions. Too often they are published without the *"why"* nor the consideration of how someone in the field might follow them.

I helped a client develop a recycling policy. The first draft had great technical detail and carried the official and formal weight of something to be taken seriously. Past the legalese speak, a person reading it for the first time would be challenged to follow it. We broke the process down and imagined ourselves in the shoes of field staff. We came up with simple step-by-step language for an infographic with an if-then style list—if the item is one of these, then do this, and if the item is one of those, then do that. Policies should always be approached in this way, with user-centered design and approachability.

How this client will accelerate sustainability becomes the ultimate test. They have a rewards program whereby staff earn points for various activities. They associate a good reward with participation in this program. If you include the *"what's in it for me?"* angle of an initiative, your recruitment will be more effective. Sure, we'd like them to participate solely out of the goodness of their heart, but it's okay if that's not enough. Other incentives are a form of empowerment, if not for the people who earn them, then for the people who invested so much in developing the policy and want so much to see good come from it. If the incentives cause people to follow through, that's a win-win.

Creating policies can be complicated because layers of approval are tricky to navigate. I suggest green teams use a reverse engineering tactic. Take something you're already doing well and formalize it into a policy.

For example, many organizations have norms in place like defaulting to double-sided printing, recycling toner cartridges, or buying paper made of post-consumer recycled content. If this has been routine for a while, many will think *"what's the big deal?"* It feels too easy to take credit for something you're already accustomed to. People assume sustainability must mean doing something drastically different and difficult; however, if you formalize a current practice into a policy, you ensure it lives on despite turnover and it eases staff into adopting other policies you put forth.

In the world of sustainability, policies check a lot of boxes. One of those boxes is to comply with a formal commitment or pledge.

PLEDGES

I use the term *"pledges"* as a catchall for any sort of public or customer-facing commitment, which range from being a signatory related to a particular cause to a far more comprehensive reporting requirement.

Customer demand may trigger executives to give the green team leader permission to take sustainability initiatives further and make them permanent. Increasingly, clients request vendors commit to frameworks or submit to one of many ESG assessment platforms. Two of the most common I encounter are EcoVadis and CDP. In both cases, submitters receive a score, which they can choose to disclose. In theory, an organization raises its score year over year, and this builds reputation and wins deals.

Ideally, leverage pledges to get staff and executives to further sustainability and to confirm for champions their work is essential to the business. It's equally important to communicate the why of commitments to staff at large. If the organization is truly dedicated to continuous improvement (for example, raising their scores), they should view this as much a commitment internally as externally. When the promises ring hollow to staff, it's not likely they can authentically represent the brand in the marketplace. If doing it to attract talent, watch out for buyers' remorse once they're inside and see all talk and no walk. In this case even the talk will sound fake and empty.

This sounds like a chicken and egg scenario. You would think one would not put out into the public sphere obligations for what one will do when sustainability still is not an official role in the organization. However, this is often how it plays out. Given the rigorous requirements of submitting to either of the aforementioned or other platforms, it's surprising so many companies go this route *before* they have staff devoted to sustainability.

As long as customers want to see a score, someone, somewhere will need to ensure initiatives are moving along. This exemplifies the power of reporting platforms. For the first few years, this can be an annual scramble to collect stories and data requested, which can prompt the implementation of a new initiative or two so the following year's report will be more impressive. It may be a side job for someone or the green team's assignment, but at some point someone in power realizes this is just too much and too important not to have anyone with an official responsibility. If the organization does not want to lose face, pledges can lead to full-time sustainability positions.

POSITIONS

If it's no one's job, then it's no one's job. In the early phases, when no one takes responsibility, it can naturally fall through the cracks. I often hear *"oh yeah, we used to blah, blah, blah. And then so-and-so left."* When the one person who tenaciously cared about sustainability leaves, when it isn't ingrained in the system and structure, don't expect the car to drive itself.

If we rely on and assume anything related to social or environmental impact is supposed to be a volunteer thing, this limits how much you can implement change. Green team, yes! But take it a step further. Start with the person who sparked all this in the first place and give them a formal position, with the weight and authority associated it deserves.

This trajectory is the most common path I see. Rarely am I conversing with people hired directly into a sustainability job. It's almost always, *"I came to do this, and I was chosen to also do that."* Pitching a new position within an organization is not easy. It's more approachable to start with an intern with a full-time focus on sustainability, or a coordinator position who shares other duties besides sustainability. Starting with a lower-level position is less risky than starting at the executive level. Not to imply entry-level staff are more expendable, but they are certainly more malleable and less expensive.

If an additional position is not feasible, consider offering the green team added incentives or pay to take on the extra burden. For many of them, being on the green team is not a burden because they are passionate about social or environmental issues. However, the responsibilities of collecting, processing, analyzing, and presenting data might be more of a load than they had been willing to carry. It can take a ton of time to do these tasks. I'm not sure outsiders appreciate how difficult ESG reporting is. It's onerous, and it's exacerbated by the fact that most companies do not collect or organize the right data in the right way.

When promoting the sustainability champion into a formal position, be careful not to assume because they are the one person doing this formally, they have all skillsets that position demands. Interns and coordinators are a great place to start but still insufficient for the sophisticated reporting required and leadership needed to drive sustainability initiatives. You need someone at the right level to ensure decision-making authority, budgetary access, influence on systems, and a greater span of control. This would be a major step toward truly integrated sustainability.

In GreenBiz's *State of Green Business 2023* report, authors from LinkedIn present statistics on growth in green jobs. They make the point that "[t]he fastest-growing Greening titles may not necessarily be obviously green, but green skills are increasingly required to succeed in these roles and their growth tells an important story."[1]

The top highest ranked skills for sustainability managers from 2015 to 2021 included program and project management and data analysis—skills needed throughout an organization for success in any program.[2] Interestingly, public speaking also appeared in this list in five of the seven years, supporting the earlier theme where enlightenment requires, or is at least greatly facilitated by, strong speaking skills.[3]

The "Greening" positions include titles like Vice President Facilities and Director of Regulatory Affairs, showing environmentalism increasingly becoming a factor in existing roles. These examples are all formal and technical in nature. As stated already, many organizations start off more elementary than that. One or a few people start the movement and eventually job descriptions and titles catch up. I make this point so executives understand acceleration requires an effort to empower champions, activate hidden passion and talent, and put serious salary and HR heft behind the maturing sustainability program.

I also want to stress to younger professionals you are not limited by the lack of an environmental or engineering degree. Most of the time, the first official position is created for the person essentially already doing the job anyway. The champion demonstrated so much value, the position followed. If you want badly to align passion with profession, and wonder how, here are common threads across champions turned professionals I've encountered over the years:

- Just be good at what you do. Focus on quality, communication, professionalism, due diligence, and problem solving. You'll get noticed. Jana wasn't selected because she happened to be in an elevator; she was selected because she'd demonstrated excellence in her work. Make it easy for a boss to empower you based on existing trust and reputation. Be the natural choice.

- Be bold and willing to take risks. This is self-empowerment. Remember, you are asking for a job most people still aren't entirely sure how to describe. Navigating unchartered territory can be daunting. Volunteer to start a green team or pilot a continuous improvement effort with a good business case.

- Join associations. This is a form of empowerment from outside your organization but within your profession or industry. You can be emboldened by what others have done at competing or peer organizations. Seek out sustainability focused associations or societies, such as the Sustainable Purchasing Leadership Council, the Green Sports Alliance, or the Society for Sustainable Events.

- Be empathetic. It's easy to think you are the one with all the needs because of your deep desire for a different career. Ultimately, though, your purpose is to serve and lead others. If you spend time learning perspectives and gaining trust, when the moment is right, you will have developed a fan base ready to support you. This gives you and your cause momentum.

- Your pain is not their pain. When trying to convince upper management, they will not care nearly as much about a particular change as you do. In the grand scheme of things, your urgency to fix recycling pales in comparison with their need to run an entire organization. Be persistent because what starts out as a pain in your side will eventually become a pain in theirs. When that happens, you'll be ready with the answer.

Every person I know who worked themselves into a sustainability role from another position put these principles into action. You know they say it's easier to get a job when you have a job. Job hunting when you're unemployed is the worst! If you are employed, give yourself the informal job of sustainability and you'll likely find it's easier to get that dream job, whether in your organization or another.

Be encouraged by the results of the 2022 *State of the Profession* report by GreenBiz and Weinreb Group. It showed only 30 percent of surveyed companies had not added staff related to ESG reporting, while 35 percent have hired more consultants, and 50 percent have hired one or more full-time employee for these roles.[4] ESG reporting is a specific knowledge and skillset but most champions I've interviewed and mentored found themselves early on having to figure out how they were going to measure and report results.

Last, if you are an organizational leader, recognize the magnitude of empowering the champion through a formal position. Ultimately, a devoted position ensures forward momentum. One champion I spoke with put it best: "With sustainability as my full-time role, it's embedded in our mission. It's not like I have to keep it alive, it's just there."

EXPONENTIAL IMPACT APPLICATION AND DISCUSSION

- What are the inflection points in your organization that are likely to trigger substantial momentum and accelerate social and environmental initiatives? Does a particular executive stakeholder need to commit? Does a key client insist on better performance in these areas? How can you leverage that to apply pressure to the gas pedal?

- Of the following, which is in place? Which are primed for a boost? What's the next step to get there?

  o   A formal green team (or other committee name) that meets consistently and takes action.

o   Policies that specifically dictate or define sustainable measures. If these are in place, how effective are they?

o   A pledge or promise to external stakeholders. Which ones have your competitors already signed up for?

o   Reporting, whether to a formal assessment platform, or just a marketing piece to impress clients.

CHAPTER 19

ACTUALIZATION: HOLISTIC INTEGRATION

FROM REALITY TO THEORY

In the previous chapter, concepts such as formalizing sustainability into a role and giving champions decision-making power might infer it is then fully integrated into the organization. However, assimilation goes to a deeper place. When writing this book, an editor suggested *"assimilation"* made him think of a sci-fi scenario, like a cyborg taking over a human. I'm comfortable with that notion when it comes to sustainability getting into the very heart and soul of an organization!

My knowledge of this phase, from a sustainability standpoint, is largely theoretical. Why? Because the very nature of my work means I guide organizations in the activation and acceleration stages. I hope, as I journey with repeat customers, to see actualization firsthand.

I can, however, draw upon my earlier career. In the nineties, technology was beginning to take over every corporate function. If you can't remember what it was like to get anywhere without a GPS, imagine trying to recall the days we didn't use spreadsheets or email (assuming you were even alive then!). The career path initially attracted those with higher levels of education from technical and scientific institutions. Eventually, skilled labor–style training and accreditation began popping up and made the industry more accessible to those with only a high school diploma.

I had speculated corporate technology roles would go the way of trades such as electricians or plumbers. These can be highly skilled and lucrative careers; however, advanced degrees are not requisite to success. To me, this democratization of technology was an important tipping point. One day, I saw this play out in a funny way when I requested someone from IT to fix a printer. A guy showed up with a toolbelt around his waist and when he bent under my desk, he exposed his butt crack, just like a plumber might.

We are headed in the same direction with sustainability. Just as with technology and software in the nineties, today many consider it elusive or incomprehensible. However, in actualized organizations, it is deeply ingrained. Every department, division, and location have an integrated manifestation of sustainability. Such organizations are typically founded on sustainability principles and have managed to keep those at their core.

Examples of such companies include Patagonia, Ben & Jerry's, Method, Tom's of Maine, and Whole Foods. Those are the ones any reader is likely to recognize; however, thousands more social enterprises exist. By no means am I suggesting they are perfect. Critics may point out these organizations are not doing enough or that they've sold their soul to a larger conglomerate (for example, Unilever bought Ben & Jerry's, Colgate-Palmolive bought Tom's of Maine, and Amazon bought Whole Foods). Nonetheless, they are closer to integrated sustainability than most organizations could hope to be.

INTEGRATION

A common saying, walk the talk, applies to arenas beyond the execution of sustainability plans. So many who aspire to work for organizations authentically carrying out a people, planet, and profit mission lament that their organizations are mostly talk, not enough walk.

As noted in reference to greenwashing, I doubt this is some nefarious scheme hatched by the board or executives to dupe the world. Most likely, the issue stems from the absence of accountability systems that would keep everyone aware and honest. After I've trained a group of people and spurred an initial excitement of embracing new practices, I later hear managers bemoan how easy it is to lose momentum. The lack of consistency and continuity kills sustainability initiatives that rely on human participation of any kind.

To ensure every department and level of the organization remains steadfast, weave the threads of social and environmental causes through the tapestry of your organization. The very organizational systems and processes that keep money flowing need to also be applied to sustainability. Rather, sustainability needs to be ingrained in strategic planning, business model design, reporting, and *culture*! Fully unpacking how sustainability integrates into those steps is too much for the scope of this book, particularly because it can be so nuanced, so here I introduce each but then drill down on elements of culture.

STRATEGIC PLANNING

Strategic planning focuses an organization and points collective efforts toward achieving the mission and goals in a way that is synergistic. When social and environmental targets are in the mix, this ensures teams do not chase all the shiny impact objects it's so tempting to pursue. Some companies' sustainability initiatives are intertwined with their overall strategy because the idea is so linked to how their product is designed, manufactured, distributed, and sold. Examples include:

- Ikea leverages its power over the supply chain to bring costs down on sustainable features, therefore passing those savings on to consumers so price is less of an inhibitor to sustainable purchases.[1]

- Kroger (a major, US-based grocery chain) has committed to protect pollinators and promote biodiversity by requiring all fresh produce suppliers to have Integrated Pest Management (IPM) by 2030.[2]

- Estée Lauder has overachieved on its supplier diversity goals and empowers decision-making throughout the organization so customization ensures more opportunities to tap into supplier alternatives to develop and deliver the products customers crave.[3]

In larger organizations, strategic planning also happens at departmental or divisional levels, so keeping everyone headed in the same direction is critical. High-level, overarching goals are translated into relevant objectives, which include classic business metrics—growth, revenue, savings, margins, market share, and productivity. These may run counter to social and environmental outcomes and, if so, we may discover sustainability is lip service or relegated to a philanthropic activity.

BUSINESS MODEL

When a business accelerates toward sustainability, strategic initiatives move to the forefront. However, this occurs almost as a happy accident, and not because the concept was baked into the strategy. When the company is actualized, sustainability becomes a filter and a magnifier within organizational planning processes. Organizations committed to a fully integrated approach to sustainability may choose to demonstrate that through a B Corp certification. The structure of the criteria is such that every element of a business is evaluated for social and environmental performance, transparency, and accountability.[4]

The business model guides how an organization earns and spends money. It shows the sources of funding and sales (or cash in) and how that cash is spent. Ultimately, sustainability may be built into the business model of the organization, and the flow of money is inextricably tied to social and environmental outcomes. Many organizations already add the cost of carbon in their business operations budgeting. This can range from investments in technologies that reduce operational emissions to earmarking funds for carbon offsets.

REPORTING

Reporting reflects the details, successes, and challenges of achieving goals and carrying out strategy. Producing sustainability reports has become common, if not required, among most global corporations. As of 2022, 90 percent of the Russell 1000® publishes ESG reports.[5] For smaller or privately held businesses, reporting on social and environmental impact remains nascent.

I find clients I work with who are just beginning to activate internal resources and put into place mechanisms that accelerate sustainability do so because they need something to report. Their customers and/or competitors have motivated them to figure out their story. In those phases, reporting is more reflecting back and asking, *"What have we done that we can report?"*

Early results tend to be qualitative and hard data difficult to come by. Data collection and analysis are no small feat, especially when few if any systems are in place to hold or handle the needed data. When helping clients put together their sustainability reports, I frequently point out, "Okay, we went through a lot of effort to pull together this number. Do you now have a system set up to track this moving forward?" Surprisingly, or not I guess, the answer is often no. Impact reporting therefore is a fire drill, not an activity that exhibits an actualized state of being.

Furthermore, benchmarking and baselines are not always present; therefore, a historical track record or awareness of what's happening in their industry precludes a reporting mindset. Measurement and reporting are an afterthought; however, eventually, it becomes a forethought. If we want something to report on next year, we should launch new initiatives now with targeted outcomes we hope to achieve.

TRANSFORMATION IN CULTURE

Each of the characterizations of maturity described above go hand in hand with an organizational culture marked by continuous improvement mindsets, organizational development supporting social and environmental causes, and formal accountability expectations and protocols.

When organizations transition from a *"check-the-box"* approach to sustainability to a culture of care that permeates, change endures, and impact becomes lasting. Earlier I shared the example of Bob's Red Mill, which chose to become a one hundred percent employee-owned business. The founder considered this the best defense to ensure his organization stayed faithful to their values and his legacy would endure.

Actualization requires accountability and ownership at all leadership levels. When managers mandate sustainability initiatives but do not even attend the training, they send a message to staff that they don't value it and won't support it. In general, when managers just dial it in, the rest of the staff in the chain of action feel downgraded in their effectiveness.

The fundamental job design should also reflect evolved values. At one convention center, the entire food donation process was taken out of the hands of department leaders and put in the hands of line-level teams. Their sense of ownership and pride was undeniable. It's vital to integrate sustainability so it's a natural and incremental element of what staff already do. If it's triggering a desire staff have anyway (which you discover with empathy), the uptake and success likely become stronger.

Roll out programs such that the default should be opting out, not opting in. This is a leap not only for those doing everyday jobs but for those introducing new tasks, typically by a green team or a newer department devoted to sustainability. They are eager and actualized but need to understand staff may not yet have caught up in this regard.

I had a conversation about measuring and tracking food waste with someone who's been pushing the sustainability envelope for decades. This person asked, "Ooh, what if we could add food miles in the calculations?" In other words, what's the distance food traveled to get there? This is frequently more than one thousand miles, so in his mind the carbon footprint of food waste represents a critical piece to highlight.

Yes, food miles and many other sustainability qualities could be factored in; but exactly whose job is it to research those details of every ingredient? Whose job is it to add food miles to a tracker spreadsheet or software platform? What support has been provided to do that efficiently and accurately? When I presented those challenges, he understood his request extended beyond the scope of practicality in the moment. However, by setting food miles goals and incorporating an executive-level expectation for such a measurement, which would be backed by an investment in resources and training, this task could become absolutely within reach.

"Ownership of initiatives is evidenced by those involved seeing it as exciting and aspirational elements of their job, not a bothersome add-on to quickly get over and done with."

One of the champions I spoke with realized this in her journey. "One thing that has been interesting is transitioning sustainability to this operations' handoff. It's rolling out projects, getting details in place, getting it implemented, and sharing everything. But there was a point where the green team and I had to let go of things a little and let them fly and flourish without us. I've noticed my project doesn't end once it's rolled out; then it's like, how do we make sure it's just the way that we do things."

Discerning what you are *not* doing well signals you've reached a hallmark of this stage. In earlier phases, you set goals, which indicates wanting to do more and better but feels more like a textbook exercise. It may be the role of a small group of people (for example, the green team or sustainability department); however, it is not truly embraced or lived out in the organization. Ownership of initiatives is evidenced by those involved seeing it as exciting and aspirational elements of their job, not a bothersome add-on to quickly get over and done with.

You can have parts of an organization actualized and others not so much. In hotels, some locations fully embrace the corporate narrative and have evidence of initiatives throughout the property. But go to a location of that same brand in a different city, and the manifestation of sustainability may look very different.

In the hotel world, what you see at a property typically has been mandated by an operating agreement between the owner of the building and the brand on the property. These agreements dictate a lot of detail—everything from what bedsheets are acceptable to decor themes and operational parameters. For a long time, sustainability was not part of these agreements. That is starting to change, especially for brands with an eco-component to their messaging and claims. Legal agreements and contracts move an organization toward institutionalizing sustainability. While it forces compliance rather than reflecting a true culture, it can put the topic in front of enough people that it begins to seep into the heart and values and show up more as concern than conformity.

EXPONENTIAL IMPACT APPLICATION AND DISCUSSION

- Identify a few books about integrated organizations you can read for inspiration. The founders of many organizations listed in this chapter wrote books that originally inspired my foray into sustainability. I recommend *The Responsible Company* and *Conscious Capitalism*. While both paint the picture of companies with idyllic origins and impact, both are also grounded in the very real challenges organizations face when they commit to wholeheartedly living out their missions.

- How does your organization's business model invite or discourage sustainable action?

- Which parts of the organization have successfully assimilated sustainability? What about their operations reveals a holistic approach to sustainability?

How can they usher other parts of the company so that collectively the organization reaches an actualized state of exponential impact?

PART 4:

ENCOURAGE

CHAPTER 20

ENCOURAGE: KEEP THE FIRE BURNING

THE ROI OF ENCOURAGEMENT

If enlightenment and empowerment get your attention, encouragement keeps it.

Sometimes the challenges we face in sustainability are legitimate operational obstacles that emerge with any new initiative and other times they are a comedy of errors. The lame excuses, ridiculous objections, and bureaucratic difficulties make one question: *"Is it even worth it?"* When champions face challenges, we must *encourage* them to respond, *"Yes, let's not give up or give in."*

Driving change can be lonely and exhausting and champions persevere, but once initiatives are in place, those who carry the torch may fatigue quickly if not reassured their work matters. This is true of any corporate endeavor, but when the person doing the heavy lifting mostly does it on a volunteer basis, as is sometimes the case with sustainability, burnout devastates both the person and the cause.

Furthermore, when a young, eager employee gets discouraged, it leaves them bruised in ways that resound throughout their career and diminishes their ability to be effective professionally. Overlay the average cost of recruiting, hiring, and onboarding staff, and the focus organizations place on the business case of employee retention, and we cannot ignore the organizational harm accompanying this personal disappointment.

Benchmark data from the Society of Human Resource Management shows the cost of recruiting to be an average of $4,700 per employee.[1] Moreover, the hard and soft costs associated with hiring a new employee is estimated to be more like two to three times that employee's annual salary![2] This does not factor in the loss of the value they bring to the table, such as increased quality and decreased costs from their efforts to reduce energy, water, and waste.

The champions are such a mighty force that if taken out of orbit, sustainability programs might just implode! Giving these folks encouragement seems like a small price to pay to keep them around and productive.

When highly motivated, we are compelled to forge ahead, overcome, and do well. We derive intrinsic motivation from pursuing what aligns with our values and brings us joy. It is most strongly associated with positive work outcomes such as being engaged and proactive on the job, as well as lower levels of counterproductive behavior, such as conflict or theft.[3]

BAKE IN ENCOURAGEMENT

Interestingly, when I asked champions to talk about which of the four Es of this book is most important or they lean into most, none of them started with *"encourage."* I had to pry out of them "What do *you* need to keep going?" This intrinsic motivation becomes so deeply ingrained and such a strong driver they may struggle to recognize their own need for support.

Paradoxically, the social impact angle of sustainability includes a focus on mental health and well-being. Work/life balance is, in theory, a hallmark of a healthy professional and something sustainability champions advocate for; however, those who most fervently champion causes sometimes do so at the detriment of their own personal well-being. They tend to be out of touch with their own needs while being so tuned into the pain of others.

Encouragement remains critical for the champion, but also for those engaged in sustainability as part of their job. They do not have the deeper intrinsic drivers the champion has, so we need to fuel the engine. The initial spark when stakeholders are engaged and enlightening messages are spread may be followed by a quick fizzle. How do we keep the momentum after everyone gets fired up?

Human resources, people or talent management, benefits management, organizational development, and the design of work play a vital role in keeping sustainability champions and operations staff energized to carry out a social or environmental purpose. Common corporate offerings these departments can leverage to achieve exponential impact include:

- Professional Development

- Employment Benefits

- Rewards and Recognition

PROFESSIONAL DEVELOPMENT

Sustainability champions may be disregarded from a professional development perspective because other organizational leaders feel unqualified to step in and offer advice. Novices at social and environmental concepts feel inadequate to offer guidance. However, they are not new to leadership, effective communication, project management, budgeting, delegating, multitasking, and other functional skills champions need. Having a development plan for them does not have to be about sustainability; it should be about the person in the job.

For example, I found leadership development in general helped younger champions who lacked delegation skills. One champion said, "I had to figure out how to move from the person on the ground actually doing the work to the person leading that work forward. The advice I received is that my leadership style naturally leans toward being a quarterback as opposed to a coach. I'm the person in the group project who wants to start immediately and get the ball rolling because it's going to bother me otherwise. I had to work on becoming better at sitting back and waiting for somebody to step up."

Even self-aware champions need feedback, guidance, and mentoring. The dearth of these in the corporate world reverberated in my conversations with young professionals over the past fifteen years. They see themselves as just a cog in a machine and wish for more personalized attention and development. Those who lead sustainability often feel they have to be superheroes and carry the weight of knowing they are regarded differently.

The hard part of the job is not figuring out the technicalities of reducing energy or finding ethically sourced products. The challenges they face are interpersonal conflict, difficult negotiations, time management, corporate bureaucracy, and budgeting. Developing these skills already exists in the professional development landscape; just make sure champions understand the value of adding them to their toolbox.

Beyond the champions, all staff need to be supported as their careers evolve to include sustainability related tasks. Even if their motivations are not altruistic, they want to learn. The *Employbridge Voice of the American Workforce Survey Report* found a significant number of employees (more than 68 percent) are willing to invest three or more hours per week to learn new skills.[4] The top reasons for that are to prepare for a new job or a promotion (just over 40 percent) and to earn more pay (more than 67 percent).[5]

EMPLOYMENT BENEFITS

Formal programs to support those who might be carrying a heavier load than others include healthcare, awards and recognition programs, perks, and incentives. Wellness programs designed to keep employees in a healthy state of mind and help them deal with stress or illness are invaluable mechanisms to ensure the person going the extra mile doesn't crash and burn.

The changemakers may be seen as superheroes, but they are, after all, human. Many of them have set an impossible standard for themselves. In earlier stages, when volunteering or voluntold, they almost always overextended. Their passion and energy pull them toward impact work; however, they are still paid, managed, and evaluated based on their actual job title.

For the collective—both the champion and all the worker bees making things move along day by day—traditional incentives are important. The WeSpire study referenced earlier also demonstrates the role of incentives, ranging from paid time off to participate, recognition and rewards, or as part of a bonus structure. Still, 42 percent of participating companies offer no incentive at all.[6] What a missed opportunity to differentiate as an employer.

Some younger professionals not only champion environmental initiatives but drive change resonating with shifts in society at large, changes organizations must increasingly accommodate through their benefits programs.

One woman shared, "I'm learning to honor my woman's cycle. There are going to be weeks when I feel like crap and unmotivated. And thankfully, the president honors work-life balance. I'm passionate to introduce menstrual days or whatever companies are calling it now for women. It's encouraging and empowering to learn about and care for my body's health."

Male champions may be on a similar journey as they choose a lifestyle that puts them in the primary childcare position. Those who are LGBTQ+ and gender neutral or fluid will have their own well-being needs. Indeed, wellness is not one-size-fits-all and should be customized based on personal preferences and circumstances. Again, not a common feature of health and wellness benefits in some organizations and another way those in sustainability roles, in their quest for encouragement and results, can drive positive change in basic corporate functions.

REWARDS AND RECOGNITION

Research supports the value of any program focused on retention. A 2022 study of healthcare workers from WorkProud demonstrated the value of recognition programs. Of those who felt recognized, 59 percent strongly agreed they would recommend their organization to others as a place to work, 64 percent said they would be happy to spend the rest of their career with their current employer, and 50 percent said they would stay with their current employer even if offered "significantly more money" somewhere else.[7]

While bonuses, salary, and other financial incentives may be difficult to work into the budget and get approved, as sustainability is integrated into an organization, it should be factored into promotion considerations and salary calculations. In the meantime, go for the low-cost option of rewarding people and the free option of recognizing them. We only need to acknowledge the value of recognition and make a formal plan to provide it.

One champion put it well when she said, "I think for people in purpose work, you're doing the right thing, but how often do you get told you're doing a good thing? It's easy for everyone to think, well, you must be on cloud nine all the time out there doing purpose work. You must be living your dream. But that doesn't mean I don't need a pat on the back once in a while."

In rewards and recognition, beware of an *"all guts, no glory"* situation for line-level staff. Make sure compliments are going to the deserving parties. Those doing the real work to make an initiative successful may not receive emails with success stories. A director or vice president gets the acclamation with insufficient, if any, acknowledgment to those on the front line making it happen.

Sustainability initiatives are not automated. It's not a matter of flipping a switch and things just happen. Executives can take the credit for the flipping of the switch, which was the go-ahead to do the initiative, and no small thing with so many objections and barriers sustainability inevitably faces.

Once the go-ahead is given, executives might be unaware of the effort required just to get people to put a plastic bottle in the right recycle bin, move it to the right collection point, and put it in the right dumpster. Those things are taken for granted. It's assumed, *"Well, it's your job, why should you be congratulated for doing your job?"*

Nurturing the individual can come from informal kudos, but formal commendations should be given for work in sustainability. Human resource offerings designed to maximize employee productivity, engagement, and health ensure the planetary caretakers are themselves cared for.

> *"Human resource offerings designed to maximize employee productivity, engagement, and health ensure the planetary caretakers are themselves cared for.*

CONVINCING IS MOTIVATING

While it's vital to have the corporate mechanisms listed above in place, many champions commented on their joy in motivating others to change behavior. This gives the champion the feeling they are not flying solo. When they discover others care, much less want to be involved, it can be a major boost!

Valerie, whom you met earlier and who manages sustainability for an entertainment company, shared, "Seeing those shifts among people who were previously super resistant, those are the things that show me what we're doing matters. That it can change minds and it can change awareness and consciousness and behavior. The person who was most resistant now carries around a reusable cutlery set everywhere he goes. Things like that just fire me up."

David said of his work driving sustainability at a convention center, "For me, it's getting someone who's not green by nature and convincing them. Showing the benefit and seeing someone else turn onto this vision of how we should operate is very fulfilling. For example, we had a chef who was a hard worker, not negative, but just there doing his job. At first I told him 'I need you to donate food.' He was like, oh my God, here comes this green guy again. Then over the years, we would get to the point where he would call me and say, 'I have a hot box full of steaks. Are you coming to get it?'"

Notice he said "years." Yes, sometimes it can take years to get everyone on board. Often champions overshoot the mark because they assume everyone is as onboard as they are. When Jana was first launching a green team, she created an agenda, reserved a conference room, and ordered green hats and custom cups with "Sustainability Squad" printed on them. The room was all set up awaiting the masses who would band together and transform the organization. Of the twenty people she personally invited, only three showed up. It's like hosting a party where our worst fear is realized and no one shows up. It sucks.

Stick with it. The next time four people will show up to that meeting. Then three more. Then ten more. People don't want to miss out on whatever this thing is you're doing. I've heard countless stories like this. It started as this sad little gathering of two or three tree huggers, but soon it grew and grew. It became the cool thing to do.

Receive comfort that you are part of a larger movement and wait patiently for the accolades that come through the changes you see in those around you. The vision inevitably entails converting others to join the cause, and when this happens, it perpetuates positive reinforcement through a growing community.

Everyone from the champion to the passive program participant needs to feel they are part of something bigger than themselves, that they are connected to humanity, and that somehow, in some way, it all matters.

EXPONENTIAL IMPACT APPLICATION AND DISCUSSION

- What professional development do the sustainability champions in your organization need? In what way are they least successful in driving change? Identify weaknesses and match them with training courses and mentoring.

- What benefits programs are in place that perhaps champions need and are not taking advantage of?

- A low-cost way to spur both champions and employees is to institute a sustainability related recognition program. Does your organization have such a program in place? If not, consider implementing one through these steps:

  o What tasks or initiatives would qualify for a nomination? Keep in mind, staff so often think it's the extremes of people handling trash or executives driving decisions. However, staff are redesigning mandatory printouts to require fewer pages, driving digitization of contracts, collecting items from the breakroom and taking them home to recycle, and so forth. Make it clear qualifying for the recognition can take on many forms.

  o What is the means by which staff can be nominated? Consider setting up a general sustainability inbox anyone in the organization can email.

  o How often will staff be recognized? Too frequently and it may lose its value, but not frequently enough and staff will fail to be inspired by the program.

o What is the form of the recognition? This can range from nominating employees for a monthly newsletter shout-out or a gift card, to an annual award complete with plaque and a formal presentation. Check with HR that you are within the ethical and contractual boundaries of the organization.

- Which staff, working to carry out programs in your organization, need encouragement? What form would that best take to motivate them to not only do the work but to go the extra mile for social and environmental impact?

CONCLUSION: MAKE IT EXPONENTIAL!

JOURNEY, NOT DESTINATION

I started this book with the premise that we need to unlock the vault in which sustainability has been placed and make it accessible for all. Every member of an organization can, and should, play at least some role in its positive social and environmental impact.

I suspect throughout this book, you saw your own journey reflected here and there—as a champion initiating change, or a dabbler wondering how you're going to respond to emerging sustainability demands, or a seasoned pro who has hit a wall and is looking for new strategies to break through.

Similarly, you, as a champion, wannabe champion, or person hoping to find and activate champions have recognized your organization's dynamic. Perhaps you have done an excellent job practicing empathy and developing relationships, but you realize the lack of agency and autonomy means you're unable to transition your personal passion to a formal program. Maybe you're a master at empowering people but you've forged ahead without first understanding vital elements of the needs and perspectives of those around you. Maybe you have successfully practiced empathy but without this new lens of sustainability, so a new round of stakeholder engagement is necessary. For others, you may have strong recognition and retention programs, but see room to grow in how you invite those on the sidelines into the game.

However you show up in this journey, you are where you're meant to be—here, learning and receiving guidance, and now ready for your next step. While there is urgency to address the world's ills, pace yourself; this is truly a journey, not a destination. Wherever your starting point, you *can* raise your efforts to the power of human potential and generate exponential impact.

It's people that make the difference. Most of the world's problems are solvable. Yes, we need more innovation and discovery to tackle the toughest problems; however, in the 80/20 vein, we can address much of it today. To get there we must involve humans.

What prevents more progress is often the messiness and complexity of working with people. Humans reveal the possibilities of love and stewardship but also stifle advancement of positive impact. These are almost parallel paths, and our goal is to widen the path of good while narrowing the path of resistance. Notice I didn't say the path of evil. That path is what it is. There is little we can do to erase evil. We should aim to make a more approachable on-ramp so the inactive masses can join in and create undeniable momentum.

We do this by practicing the four themes covered in this book.

EMPATHY

We start by understanding what hinders those who thwart progress, knowing what makes hearts beat, and what greases the wheels of power. Empathy requires engaging a range of stakeholders, starting with yourself and your team. Don't discount the importance of your own perspective in achieving impact.

Draw in those within the entire ecosystem of your organization; however, don't get bogged down in thinking you have to check every box or please every person. It is an iterative journey, an ongoing conversation, not a transaction. Lean heavily on the cadre of consultants and experts ready and willing to expedite and magnify your organization's potential positive impact.

ENLIGHTENMENT

When we enlighten people, we make it clear what is needed, why it's necessary for a prosperous and just world, and how they can be involved. Raising awareness is a spark igniting the flame of response and action, if not passionate commitment, among staff. Those who do the work are those who *do* the work. The more they are compelled to contribute, the closer you get to exponential impact.

Communication, instruction, and reinforcement of the social and environmental aims ensure staff are connected to the heartbeat of the mission. The sustainability messaging, packaged for effective and engaging delivery, should overlay the existing operational system.

EMPOWERMENT

After we do all of the above, we need to walk the talk. This requires practical methods to carry out the work. The car is on but in idle until you make the position official and full-time. Then you step on the gas, knowing a champion is at the wheel who is equipped and supported.

Empowerment goes from an advocate who germinates out of their own self-will and spreads to others waiting for just this opportunity to come along. The progression continues to a place of actualization where sustainability is institutionalized into the processes and ingrained in the very soul of an organization.

ENCOURAGEMENT

Like anything worth pursuing in life, it's an uphill battle. Transformational work is not conducive to shortcuts, so we need support systems that generate stamina, momentum, and loyalty. Although the shortest section of the book, keeping people motivated is a critical part of the equation. As your organization approaches actualization, the mechanisms for motivation become more naturally entrenched. Nonetheless, the champions will always carry a bigger load, feel a greater burden, and need special consideration and rewards.

EXPONENTIAL IMPACT

Authentic and meaningful sustainability programs, designed and implemented with these engagement principles, elevate brands, drive efficiency, spur innovation, improve culture, change lives, protect habitats, and inspire others to do the same.

Implementing these principles requires intentionality, not lip service. They need to be fueled by positivity and culminate in experiences that deepen staff's connection with the organization, each other, the community, and the planet.

The concept of exponential is one thing being raised to the power of something else. It resonates with *"the whole is greater than the sum of the parts."* You and your organization are the parts, staff and other stakeholders are the parts of the equation that make the difference. Together, you are exponential!

ACKNOWLEDGMENTS

Writing a book is a labor of love and to achieve this, one must be fortified by the love of others. I dreamed from an early age I would be a thought leader and publish a book. My mom (Marcianne) was always my greatest cheerleader and instilled in me that I could do anything. She paved the way for me to live as a courageous woman. The rock of our family and the man from whom I inherited an entrepreneurial spirit, my father (Drexel) has always made it possible for me to land on my feet when the economy or life's crap dealt me a bad hand. I'm eternally grateful for that foundation and safety net because without it, I would not have had the bandwidth to pursue a lifelong dream. My sister (Deeann), the funniest person I know, just gets me and always helps me remember the good stuff in life.

Friends who have been such an important part of my journey:

Laurie Green for being what I need when I need it for nearly thirty years, Elizabeth Lambrides for hours and hours sitting around solving the world's problems, Diana Catalina Beltran for validating me from our first encounter and continuing to believe in and promote Astrapto, Mariela Bazán for being a great partner in the work of sustainability and a lifesaver during the pandemic, Katharine Barrantes for being a master at travel itineraries and outdoor adventures, Chance Thompson for showing me other angles when I become myopic, Phil Mott for welcoming me into the world of hospitality, Joan Plisko for your beautiful soul, Rick Garlick for your generous spirit, and Irene Lane for being an excellent collaborator.

I have had the great fortune of working with some amazing clients. I do not take lightly the trust they have put in me and my team to deliver exponential impact on their behalf. Thank you Pete Pearson (and your team) for Astrapto's first big break and your ongoing faith in our work, Molly Crouch for being my hilarious guide into the world of catering and a dear friend to boot, Mac Campbell for being an all-around amazing human being, and others including Benoit Sauvage, Donna Brokowski, Paul Pellizzari, Lindsay Pearson, Kristen Fulmer, Ariane Hiltebrand, and Marianne Schmidhofer.

Those listed above have inspired me with their stories of sustainability and intrapreneurship, but my life is rich with other friends and acquaintances whose achievements in sustainability and entrepreneurship have influenced and inspired me: Vivian Hunter, Tracy Stuckrath, Jana Brooks, Claudia van't Hullenaar, Ali Cammisa, Zoe Moore, Katrina Klett, Amy Spatrisano, Rachel Foster, Amanda Britt, Suzanne Morrell, Kate Cardoso, Sammy Davies, Elaine Alberts, Ryan Green, Gina Marotta, Ann Zald, Amy Jiang, LeVincia Porch, Alex Boyd, David Fiss,

Paul Salinger, Jody Brandes, James Filtz, Rob Watson, Sue Tinnish, Lori McKinney, Kim Bryden, and Michele Fox.

Other early book supporters include: Hannah Womer, Joe While, Andrea Blood, Jennifer Storey, Fredrik Axelsson, Sarah Schu, Owen Chiu, LauraAnne Brown, Horst Bayer, Kris Coperine, Donna Rogers, Patty Simonton, Josh Adams, John Bushman, and Alejandra Hierro.

Many contributed to my book journey—from cover design ideas from Alexa Martinez to the whole Manuscripts team, but I'm particularly grateful for Eric Koester for putting together a program making it possible for so many to achieve their publishing ambitions, Sherman Morrison for doing me a solid with my research efforts, Reannon Muth for patiently enduring my endless excuses for not focusing on book marketing, and Carol McKibben for making the editing process much less painful than I'd anticipated.

Last but not least, I am a spiritual being and I give gratitude to God for the wisdom, insights, and words that came together with this beautiful energy I pray now goes out into the world and perpetuates exponential impact.

NOTES

INTRODUCTION

1. Department of Economic and Social Affairs, "The 17 Goals—SDG Knowledge," *United Nations Department of Economic and Social Affairs* (blog), United Nations, Accessed March 11, 2024, https://sdgs.un.org/goals.

2. Dr. Aurora Dawn Benton, *Go Rogue! A Supplier Diversity Mandate for Events Industry Professionals*, (San Francisco: Society for Sustainable Events and Astrapto, 2022), https://www.astrapto.com/s/GO-ROGUE-a-Supplier-Diversity-Mandate-April2022-FINAL.pdf.

3. Ellen Weinreb, *State of the Profession 2022* (Oakland, California: GreenBiz, 2022), 9, https://www.greenbiz.com/report/state-profession-2022-report.

CHAPTER 1. THE SUSTAINABILITY SCENE

1. Department of Economics and Social Affairs, "The 17 Goals—SDG Knowledge," *United Nations Department of Economic and Social Affairs* (blog), *United Nations*, Accessed March 11, 2024, https://sdgs.un.org/goals.

2. United Nations, "17 Goals to Transform our World," Home, Welcome to the United Nations—Sustainable

Development Goals, Accessed March 25, 2024, https://www.un.org/sustainabledevelopment/.

3. Fernando Trías de Bes, *The Little Black Book of Entrepreneurship: A Contrarian's Guide to Succeeding Where Others Have Failed* (Berkeley, California: Ten Speed Press, 2008), 74.

4. US Department of Labor, *Child Labor in the Production of Cocoa*, (Washington, DC: Bureau of International Labor Affairs, 2020), https://www.dol.gov/agencies/ilab/our-work/child-forced-labor-trafficking/child-labor-cocoa.

5. John Dumay, Cristiana Bernardi, Samuel Mawutor, and Stephanie Perkiss, "At Chocolate Time, We've Discovered What the Brands That Score Best on Child Labour and the Environment Have in Common," *Economy* (blog), *The Conversation*, March 7, 2023, https://theconversation.com/at-chocolate-time-weve-discovered-what-the-brands-that-score-best-on-child-labour-and-the-environment-have-in-common-201682.

CHAPTER 2. EMPATHIZE: LAY THE FOUNDATION

1. IDEO Staff, "What Is Human-Centered Design?" *Design Kit*, IDEO, Accessed March 8, 2024, https://www.designkit.org/human-centered-design.html.

2. John Broadway, "The Stories We Tell to Tell Other Stories: Remember People in Sustainability Reporting,"

Sustainable Brands (blog), July 2023, https://sustainablebrands.com/read/marketing-and-comms/stories-remember-people-sustainability-reporting.

3. Yogi Staff, *"Yogi Annual Sustainability Report,"* Yogi Annual Sustainability Report (blog), *Yogi*, 2024, https://yogiproducts.com/2023/10/yogi-annual-sustainability-report/.

4. UNICEF, *An Evaluation of the PlayPump ® Water System as an Appropriate Technology for Water, Sanitation and Hygiene Programmes* (New York: UNICEF, October 2007), https://www-tc.pbs.org/frontlineworld/stories/southernafrica904/flash/pdf/unicef_pp_report.pdf.

5. Nitika Johri, "The Importance of a Human-Centered Approach in Implementing the Sustainable Development Goals," *Center for American Progress* (blog), September 14, 2016, https://www.americanprogress.org/article/the-importance-of-a-human-centered-approach-in-implementing-the-sustainable-development-goals/.

6. Ibid.

7. Jamie Ballard, "Women Are More Likely Than Men To Say They're a People-Pleaser, and Many Dislike Being Seen As One," *YouGov*, August 22, 2022, https://today.yougov.com/society/articles/43498-women-more-likely-men-people-pleasing-poll.

8. Susan Hunt Stevens, "State of ESG Employee Engagement 2023," *Research and Reports* (blog), *WeSpire*, April 29, 2023, https://www.wespire.com/blog/state-of-esg-employee-engagement.

9. John Davies, *State of Green Business 2023* (Oakland: GreenBiz, January 2023), https://www.greenbiz.com/report/state-green-business-2023, 19.

10. Department of Economic and Social Affairs, "Goal 16: Promote Peaceful and Inclusive Societies for Sustainable Development, Provide Access to Justice for All and Build Effective, Accountable and Inclusive Institutions at All Levels," *United Nations Department of Economic and Social Affairs (blog)*, United Nations, Accessed March 11, 2024, https://sdgs.un.org/goals/goal16#targets_and_indicators.

11. Department of Economic and Social Affairs, "Goal 13: Take Urgent Action to Combat Climate Change and Its Impacts," *United Nations Department of Economic and Social Affairs (blog)*, United Nations, Accessed March 11, 2024, https://sdgs.un.org/goals/goal13#targets_and_indicators.

12. United Nations Department of Economic and Social Affairs, *Goal 5: Achieve Gender Equality and Empower All Women and Girls* (New York: United Nations, 2023), https://sdgs.un.org/goals/goal5#targets_and_indicators.

13. Jemima McEvoy, "Eskimo Pie Becomes Edy's Pie: Here are all the Brands that are Changing Racist

Names and Packaging," *Forbes*, October 2020, https://www.forbes.com/sites/jemimamcevoy/2020/10/06/eskimo-pie-becomes-edys-pie-here-are-all-the-brands-that-are-changing-racist-names-and-packaging/?sh=50c7385b56a7.

CHAPTER 3. INSIDE: THE HEART OF THE MATTER

1. Ocean Conservancy Staff, "Ocean Conservancy Endorses Newly Introduced Farewell to Foam Act in Wake of 'What the Foam?!' Campaign Launch," *Newsroom: A Voice for our Ocean (blog), Ocean Conservancy*, December 7, 2023, https://oceanconservancy.org/news/ocean-conservancy-endorses-newly-introduced-farewell-to-foam-act-in-wake-of-what-the-foam-campaign-launch/.

2. Environmental Working Group, "What is Styrene?," *EWG's Skin Deep, Environmental Working Group*, Accessed March 11, 2024, https://www.ewg.org/skindeep/ingredients/726276-STYRENE/.

3. Edelman, *Edelman Trust Barometer 2023 Survey Report* (Chicago, Illinois: Edelman, 2023), 16, 21, https://www.edelman.com/trust/2023/trust-barometer.

4. Ibid.

5. Katty Kay and Claire Shipman, *The Confidence Code: The Science and Art of Self-Assurance—What Women Should Know* (New York City: Harper Business, 2014).

6. Gallup, "CliftonStrengths Online Talent Assessment," *CliftonStrengths Online Talent Assessment, Gallup*, Accessed March 11, 2024, https://www.gallup.com/cliftonstrengths/en/252137/home.aspx.

CHAPTER 4. OUTSIDE: PEOPLE AND PLANET AS STAKEHOLDERS

1. Ros Davidson, "The Environmental Impact of Cut Flowers? Not so Rosy," *We Humans* (blog), IDEAS.*TED*, May 5, 2021, https://ideas.ted.com/the-environmental-impact-of-cut-flowers-not-so-rosy/.

2. Eunice Waweru, "The Dark Side of the Flower Sector: the Growing Exploitation of Women in Kenya," *Blog (blog), Anti-Slavery International*, November 3, 2022, https://www.antislavery.org/latest/flower-sector-exploitation-of-women-in-kenya/.

3. Ibid.

4. Claire Cho, "Where do Your Flowers Come From? The Thorns of the Colombian Cut Flower Industry," *Novel Hand* (blog), June 25, 2021, https://novelhand.com/colombian-cut-flower-industry/.

5. Sarah Anderson, "Environmental Benefits of Local Cut Flower Production," *Department of Horticultural Science* (blog), *University of Minnesota*, February 16, 2023, https://horticulture.umn.edu/news/local-cut-flower-production.

6. Ros Davidson, "The Environmental Impact of Cut Flowers? Not so Rosy," *We Humans* (blog), IDEAS.*TED*, May 5, 2021, https://ideas.ted.com/the-environmental-impact-of-cut-flowers-not-so-rosy/.

7. Nick Saraceni, "Bridging the Gap Between Donations and Meaningful Connections," *Triple Pundit, Subaru of America*, February 6, 2024, https://www.triplepundit.com/story/2024/philanthropy-donations-connections/794276.

CHAPTER 5. UP: EXECUTIVE VIEWPOINT

1. Dave Armon, "United Airlines CEO's Straight Talk on Sustainability Irks Competitors," *Triple Pundit* (blog), April 19, 2022, https://www.triplepundit.com/story/2022/united-airlines-ceo-sustainability/741991.

2. Bob Willard, "Free, Open-Source Tools for Sustainability Champions," *Sustainability Advantage*, Accessed March 14, 2024, https://sustainabilityadvantage.com/.

CHAPTER 6. DOWN: THE FRONT LINES OF IMPACT

1. IDEO, "Experts on the Front Lines," *IDEO* (blog), Accessed March 19, 2024, https://www.ideo.com/works/ford-foundation.

2. Employbridge, *17th Annual Voice of the American Workforce Survey Report* (Duluth, Georgia: Employbridge, 2023), https://www.employbridge.com/voice-of-the-american-workforce/.

3. Ibid.

4. Employbridge, *17th Annual Voice of the American Workforce Survey Report* (Duluth, Georgia: Employbridge, 2023), https://www.employbridge.com/voice-of-the-american-workforce/.

5. Matt Gonzales, "The Plight of Frontline Workers," *All Things Work* (blog), *SHRM*. January 13, 2023, https://www.shrm.org/topics-tools/news/all-things-work/plight-front-line-workers.

6. Bob's Red Mill Staff, "Proudly Employee Owned Since 2010," Proudly Employee Owned, Bob's Red Mill, Accessed March 19, 2024, https://www.bobsredmill.com/employee-owned.

7. Joseph Blasi and Douglas Kruse, *Employee Ownership and ESOPs: What We Know from Recent Research* (New York, New York: Aspen Institute, 2023), 3, https://www.aspeninstitute.org/publications/employee-ownership-and-esops-what-we-know-from-recent-research/.

8. Ibid.

9. Joseph Blasi and Douglas Kruse, *Employee Ownership and ESOPs: What We Know from Recent Research* (New

York, New York: Aspen Institute, 2023), 4, https://www.
aspeninstitute.org/publications/employee-ownership-
and-esops-what-we-know-from-recent-research/.

10. Employee Ownership Foundation and Rutgers School
of Management and Labor Relations, *Employee-Owned
Firms in the COVID-19 Pandemic* (Washington, DC:
Employee Ownership Foundation, 2023), 4, https://
www.employeeownershipfoundation.org/research/
employee-owned-firms-excel-at-employee-retention-
during-pandemic.

11. Susan Hunt Stevens, "State of Employee Engagement
in Impact," *Research and Reports* (blog), *WeSpire*,
April 29, 2023, https://www.wespire.com/blog/
state-of-esg-employee-engagement.

12. Ibid.

CHAPTER 7. AROUND: ORGANIZATIONAL CULTURE

1. Jim Harter, "US Employee Engagement Needs a
Rebound in 2023," *Workplace* (blog), *Gallup*, January
25, 2023, https://www.gallup.com/workplace/468233/
employee-engagement-needs-rebound-2023.aspx.

2. Ibid.

3. Henkel, "Waste Not: Henkel North America
Operations Sites Embrace Zero Production Waste

to Landfill Initiative," *Sustainability* (blog), *3BLCSRwire*, January 26, 2024, https://www. csrwire.com/press_releases/793571-waste-not-henkel-north-america-operations-sites-embrace-zero-production-waste.

4. Ibid.

5. Henkel, "Waste Not: Henkel North America Operations Sites Embrace Zero Production Waste to Landfill Initiative," *Sustainability* (blog), *3BLCSRwire*, January 26, 2024, https://www. csrwire.com/press_releases/793571-waste-not-henkel-north-america-operations-sites-embrace-zero-production-waste.

CHAPTER 8. ACROSS: STRENGTH IN NUMBERS

1. Edelman, *Edelman Trust Barometer 2023 Survey Report* (Chicago, Illinois: Edelman, 2023), 16, 21, https://www.edelman.com/trust/2023/trust-barometer.

2. Pacific Coast Collaborative Staff, "Help Us Cut Food Waste in Half by 2030," *Reducing Wasted Food* (blog), *Pacific Coast Collaborative*, Accessed March 25, 2024, https://pacificcoastcollaborative.org/food-waste/.

CHAPTER 9. ACROSS: AN EXTENSION OF THE FAMILY

1. Ellen Weinreb, *State of the Profession 2022* (Oakland, California: GreenBiz, 2022), 12, https://www. greenbiz.com/report/state-profession-2022-report.

CHAPTER 10. ENLIGHTEN: PRECURSOR TO IMPACT

1. Employbridge, *17th Annual Voice of the American Workforce Survey Report* (Duluth, Georgia: Employbridge, 2023), 6, https://www.employbridge. com/voice-of-the-american-workforce/.

CHAPTER 11. WHO: IT TAKES ALL KINDS

1. Susan Hunt Stevens, "State of ESG Employee Engagement 2023," *Research and Reports* (blog), *WeSpire*, April 29, 2023, https://www.wespire.com/ blog/state-of-esg-employee-engagement.

2. Ibid.

3. Gina Gambetta, "RI IWD 2023 Survey: Why is Finance Still Failing Women?," *Hot Topics* (blog), *Responsible Investor*, March 8, 2023, https://www. responsible-investor.com/ri-iwd-2023-survey-why-is-finance-still-failing-women/.

1. Eastman, *2023 Consumer Insights Report* (Kingsport, TN: Eastman, 2023), 4, https://www.greenbiz.com/report/eastman-2023-consumer-insights-report.

2. United Nations, "Greenwashing—The Deceptive Tactics Behind Environmental Claims," *Climate Action* (blog), *United Nations*, Accessed April 10, 2024, https://www.un.org/en/climatechange/science/climate-issues/greenwashing.

3. RepRisk, *On the Rise: Navigating the Wave of Greenwashing and Social Washing* (Zurich: RepRisk, October, 2023), https://www.reprisk.com/news-research/reports/on-the-rise-navigating-the-wave-of-greenwashing-and-social-washing.

4. Ibid.

5. Simone Preuss, "H&M's Response to Allegations of Dumping Textile Waste in Global South Highlights Industry's Problems," *Business* (blog), *Fashion United*, June 28, 2023, https://fashionunited.com/news/business/h-m-s-response-to-allegations-of-dumping-textile-waste-in-global-south-highlights-industry-s-problems/2023062854563.

6. Truth in Advertising, "Cascade Platinum," *Truth in Advertising Ad Alert* (blog), June 30, 2020, https://truthinadvertising.org/articles/cascade-platinum/.

7. Dan Flynn, "'Product of USA' to Mean Something Again," *Food Safety News* (blog), March 7, 2023, https://www.foodsafetynews.com/2023/03/product-of-usa-to-mean-something-again/.

8. ReFED, "In the US, 38 Percent of All Food Goes Unsold or Uneaten—and Most of That Goes to Waste," *The Problem, ReFED*, Accessed April 10, 2024, https://refed.org/food-waste/the-problem/.

9. Ibid.

10. Food and Agriculture Organization of the United Nations, "Reducing Food Loss and Waste Is Critical to Achieving a Sustainable World," YouTube, October 15, 2019, 2:43, https://www.youtube.com/watch?v=H_YjtkKTguo.

11. Joseph Poore and Thomas Nemecek, *Freshwater Withdrawals per Kilogram of Food Product* (Oxford, England: Our World in Data, 2018), https://ourworldindata.org/grapher/water-withdrawals-per-kg-poore.

CHAPTER 13. WHERE AND WHEN: GETTING THE WORD OUT

1. Employbridge, *17th Annual Voice of the American Workforce Survey Report* (Duluth, Georgia: Employbridge, 2023), 8, https://www.employbridge.com/voice-of-the-american-workforce/.

2. Susan Hunt Stevens, "State of ESG Employee Engagement 2023," *Research and Reports* (blog), *WeSpire*, April 29, 2023, https://www.wespire.com/blog/state-of-esg-employee-engagement.

3. Ibid.

CHAPTER 14. HOW: STICK THE LANDING

1. Coldplay, "Emissions Update" *Music of the Spheres World Tour*, Coldplay, June 2, 2023, https://sustainability.coldplay.com/.

2. University of Oxford, "What is Net Zero?", *Net Zero Climate* (blog), Accessed April 26, 2024, https://netzeroclimate.org/what-is-net-zero-2/.

3. Jessica Blythe, Julia Baird, Nathan Bennett, Gillian Dale, Kirsty L. Nash, Gary Pickering, and Colette C. C. Wabnitz, "Fostering Ocean Empathy Through Future Scenarios," *People and Nature*, 3, no. 6 (September 2021), ttps://doi.org/10.1002/pan3.10253.

4. Ibid.

5. Derek Sivers, "How to Start a Movement," February 2010, Long Beach, California, *TED2010*, 2:52, https://www.ted.com/talks/derek_sivers_how_to_start_a_movement.

CHAPTER 15. EMPOWER: WALK THE TALK

1. Lior Arussy, "Empowerment to Say 'No' Is a Culture (A Really Bad One)," *Chief Executive*, Accessed May 5, 2024, https://chiefexecutive.net/empowerment-to-say-no-is-a-culture-a-really-bad-one/.

2. Ibid.

CHAPTER 16: AGENCY AND AUTONOMY: CHAMPIONS RISE UP

1. Korn Ferry, "Korn Ferry Survey Reveals Impact of Return-to-Office Mandates," *Korn Ferry* (blog), April 25, 2023, https://www.kornferry.com/about-us/press/korn-ferry-survey-reveals-impact-of-return-to-office-mandates.

2. Julia Milner, "Could You Be a Victim of Micromanagement? Seven Tips to Take Back Control," *The Conversation* (blog), July 17, 2023, https://theconversation.com/could-you-be-a-victim-of-micromanagement-seven-tips-to-take-back-control-209625.

3. Harry E. Chambers, *My Way or the Highway: The Micromanagement Survival Guide* (San Francisco, California: Berrett-Koehler Publishers, 2004).

CHAPTER 17. ACTIVATION: RALLY THE TROOPS

1. Jim Harter, "US Employee Engagement Needs a Rebound in 2023," *Workplace* (blog), *Gallup*, January 25, 2023, https://www.gallup.com/workplace/468233/ employee-engagement-needs-rebound-2023.aspx.

2. Ibid.

3. LHH, *The Readiness Index* (Zurich, Switzerland: LHH, 2022), 7, https://www.cowryconsulting.com/ case-studies/lhh-readiness-index.

4. LHH, *The Readiness Index* (Zurich, Switzerland: LHH, 2022), 9, https://www.cowryconsulting.com/ case-studies/lhh-readiness-index.

5. LHH, *The Readiness Index* (Zurich, Switzerland: LHH, 2022), https://www.cowryconsulting.com/ case-studies/lhh-readiness-index.

6. Ibid.

7. Jonathan Watts, "Greta Thunberg, Schoolgirl Climate Change Warrior: 'Some People Can Let Things Go. I Can't,'" *The Guardian*, March 11, 2019, https:// www.theguardian.com/world/2019/mar/11/greta-thunberg-schoolgirl-climate-change-warrior-some-people-can-let-things-go-i-cant.

CHAPTER 18. ACCELERATION: SPEEDING UP SUSTAINABILITY

1. Peggy Brannigan and Efrem Bycer, *State of Green Business 2023: The State of Jobs and Careers* (Oakland: GreenBiz, 2023), 8-11, https://www.greenbiz.com/report/state-green-business-2023.

2. Ibid.

3. Peggy Brannigan and Efrem Bycer, *State of Green Business 2023: The State of Jobs and Careers* (Oakland: GreenBiz, 2023), 8-10, https://www.greenbiz.com/report/state-green-business-2023.

4. Ellen Weinreb, *State of the Profession 2022* (Oakland, California: GreenBiz, 2022), 12, https://www.greenbiz.com/report/state-profession-2022-report.

CHAPTER 19. ACTUALIZATION: HOLISTIC INTEGRATION

1. Heather Clancy, "How Ikea Convinces Consumers to be Green," *Climate Pioneers* (blog), *GreenBiz*, May 6, 2024, https://www.greenbiz.com/article/ikea-guiding-its-customers-toward-sustainable-consumption-heres-how.

2. Sustainable Brands Staff, "Kroger Becomes Latest Retailer to Protect Biodiversity," *Sustainable Brands*

(blog), February 2024, https://sustainablebrands.com/read/kroger-latest-retailer-protect-biodiversity.

3. Amy Brown, "How Estée Lauder Blew Past Its Supplier Diversity Goals," *Triple Pundit* (blog), December 14, 2023, https://www.triplepundit.com/story/2023/estee-lauder-supplier-diversity/791021.

4. B Lab, "About B Corp Certification—Measuring a Company's Entire Social and Environmental Impact," *B Corp*, October 6, 2023, https://www.bcorporation.net/en-us/certification/.

5. Governance and Accountability Institute, *Sustainability Reporting in Focus: New Research Shows Mid-Cap US Public Companies Closing Sustainability Reporting Gap 2022* (New York: Governance and Accountability Institute, 2023), 4, https://www.ga-institute.com/research/ga-research-directory/sustainability-reporting-trends/2023-sustainability-reporting-in-focus.html.

CHAPTER 20. ENCOURAGE: KEEP THE FIRE BURNING

1. Katie Navarra, "The Real Cost of Recruitment," *News* (blog), *SHRM*, April 11, 2022, https://www.shrm.org/topics-tools/news/talent-acquisition/real-costs-recruitment.

2. Ibid.

3. Anga Van den Broeck, Joshua L. Howard, Yves Van Vaerenbergh, Hannes Leroy, and Marylène Gagné, "Beyond Intrinsic and Extrinsic Motivation: A Meta-Analysis on Self-Determination Theory's Multidimensional Conceptualization of Work Motivation," *Organizational Psychology Review* 11, 3 (April 2021): 240-273, https://doi.org/10.1177/20413866211006173.

4. Employbridge, *17th Annual Voice of the American Workforce Survey Report* (Duluth, Georgia: Employbridge, 2023), 8, https://www.employbridge. com/voice-of-the-american-workforce/.

5. Ibid.

6. Susan Hunt Stevens, "State of ESG Employee Engagement 2023," *Research and Reports* (blog), *WeSpire*, April 29, 2023, https://www.wespire.com/ blog/state-of-esg-employee-engagement.

7. Rick Garlick, PhD, *A Case Study in Healthcare: The Monetary Impact of Employee Recognition on Employee Retention* (Dallas, Texas: WorkProud, 2023), 2, https:// go.workproud.com/l/924362/2023-01-16/3srfp5/924362/ 1673909998dRpp47d2/Monetary_Impact_of_Employee_ Recognition.pdf.